# Love Her As She Is

Jen

Please know that your
love of work makes a positive
difference—in moments &
with those you'd never
imagine. Blessings
Patricia
March 4/08

Published by Light Hearted Concepts

1411 – 25A Street S.W., Calgary, Alberta, Canada  T3C 1J8
*phone*: (403) 242•7796 — *fax*: (403) 240•1964
*e-mail*: patricia@lightheartedconcepts.com
*internet*: www.lightheartedconcepts.com

**Library and Archives Canada Cataloguing in Publication**
Morgan, Pat, 1946 –
    Love her as she is : lessons from a daughter stolen by addictions / Patricia Morgan ; with Kelly Morgan. — 2nd ed.

Includes bibliographical references.
ISBN: 0 – 9684585 – 3 – X

    1. Morgan, Pat, 1946 –. 2. Narcotic addicts — Family relationships.
3. Alcoholics — Family relationships. 4. Parents of narcotic addicts — Biography.
5. Parents of alcoholics —Biography. I. Morgan, Kelly, 1968 – II. Title.

HV5824. W6M67  2004          362.29'092'2          C2004 – 903998 – 9

Cover and interior design: Jeremy Drought, *Last Impression Publishing Service*,
    Calgary, Alberta
Interior photographs: family collection of the authors
Author photograph: *Crystal Image Photography*
Cover drawing: anonymous street sketch artist
Printed and bound in Canada by *Houghton Boston*, Saskatoon, Saskatchewan

# Love Her As She Is

## Lessons from a Daughter Stolen by Addictions

Patricia Morgan, MA
with Kelly Morgan

# Dedication

To Mary McLaughlin, Kelly's grandmother, who has demonstrated loving acceptance to three generations of young people.

To James, Danielle and Eric, Kelly's children who give extra hope and meaning to all that has happened.

# Acknowledgements in Gratitude

M Y FIRST APPRECIATION GOES TO KELLY, who sparked my desire to write letters and to more wisely choose my actions and words, and who eventually, supported and contributed to the writing of this book. She generously offered to disclose some long unshared feelings, thoughts and behaviours. Consequently, her participation in telling our story provided mutual healing and evolving.

The first edition could not have happened without Dr. Teeya Scholten; friends Linda and Joe White; journalist Joanne Good; Peter Baylis and the volunteers of the Youth Drug Line, Distress Centre/Drug Centre of Calgary; parent educator, Jean Illsley Clarke, who gave permission for her developmental affirmations to be reprinted; Kathryn MacDonell for her fine editing; Edna Gilbert for proofing; and healer Gwendolyn Jansma, who encouraged me to rewrite the manuscript with "love for yourself." My family including Les, my husband; Ben, our son; Katie, our youngest daughter; and Mary, my mother; has provided steadfast encouragement.

Wise and supportive therapists in Kelly's and my life have stimulated our personal awareness and healthy growth. Kelly appreciates Daniel Cahill, Mickey Sloot and, especially, Eva Appleyard. I feel blessed to have had Carol Hechtenthal, Ken Martin and Maria Joiner as my main therapists.

This second edition is updated and improved with the help and involvement of Edna Gilbert, Ria Meronek and Elissa Oman, who used their keen proofreading and editing eyes. While the first edition was my "homemade" effort, this new edition has the visual flair of book designer, Jeremy Drought of Last Impression Publishing Service.

**Note**: In the following pages some names have been changed for anonymity.

Wherever I roam
Though far from my home
The mother is calling her child

(from a Welsh song)

# Contents

# Introduction

THE RED MAILBOX MADE ITS USUAL ANNOYING AND CLANKING SOUND as I opened it to dispense my hundredth or more letter to Kelly. I hesitated, and really felt the frustration, disappointment and anger at sending off yet another letter with very little response. For close to eight years I had attempted to stay in contact with our daughter, Kelly—a potentially beautiful, bright and vibrant young woman. Since she had left home at sixteen years of age, she had felt lost to our family, entering a world of drugs, crime and prison. Alcohol, drugs and street life had become a daily routine for her. In that moment of hesitation I thought, "I've had it!" Then I heard a clear whisper of direction telling me what I must do. "You are not the only person struggling with a kid lost in addictions. Do something with your worry." I concluded that if I could learn how to effectively connect to Kelly, my story could, one day, be of help to others. That morning I decided to photocopy my letters before mailing them.

This book began with my collection of one way correspondence with one miraculous exception. The timing of the disclosure of these letters depended on Kelly's death or her decision to get help. The time is now here.

It has taken years for me to have acceptance and compassion for my shortcomings and to develop real compassion for Kelly's rough beginnings and consequently tough life. Kelly and I have revealed what we believe would be helpful to others who are struggling with similar issues. Although the main theme of this book is learning to love someone with addictions unconditionally, I have grappled with adopting an older child, the challenges of parenting a child with undiagnosed Attention Deficit Hyperactivity Disorder, and family of origin pain and anger. There are many "if only"s and "I wish I had"s but, there are also many lessons learned. Kelly and I have learned valuable lessons from one another and continue to do so today. We gained by identifying the painful, sometimes abusive and sometimes negligent moments, apologizing, committing to something better and then moving forward. In essence I slowly *came clean* with Kelly, and she with me.

Coming clean for an addict is much easier when the rest of the players in the addict's life take responsibility and disclose their own truths, saying, "When I hit you, hurt you, abandoned you, invaded you, humiliated you or shamed you, that was about me, not you. You were an innocent child." That doesn't negate the need for all kinds of work and changes to be made by the adult addict herself.

You will read how I learned to love myself and consequently learned to love Kelly as she is. I have made hurtful mistakes along the way and have come to a place of healing and self-acceptance. Whether Kelly entered treatment or not was about her path. In order for me to learn to love her as I desired, I needed to love myself as is. I call Kelly my main teacher because my relationship with her has deepened me.

There are too many parents who have decided their lives have been ruined because their children were stolen by addictions. If possible those parents need to take action with an intervention process to get them into treatment. However, if as in my family's case, with Kelly incredibly unavailable, it is best for parents to become as healthy and resilient as possible. Teens use an appropriate phrase— "get a life." Then, if and when their young people decide to turn around, they will see the faces of compassionate, steady and resourceful parents. That is the journey that unfolded for me, and my health became Kelly's anchor once she decided to get well.

I have learned that staying clean and clear is an ongoing process. The healthier Kelly becomes, the more she recognizes my strengths and confronts me with my failures…and her own. I feel most fortunate she has recognized that I did the best I could as a mother and she has graciously seen me as deserving a second chance to embrace her. Whether you find our sharing heartwarming or brutally honest, we offer an inside story from two different perspectives: a mother's and a daughter's. We have strengthened our wounded and broken places and are stronger in our strength— strong enough to tell our story.

# 1
# ...ten years with Kelly

I N 1973, MY HUSBAND LES AND I ADOPTED five and half year old Kelly Ann Evoy. Our biological son, Benjamin, was two years old. Kelly joined our family after a number of foster home placements and a failed adoption. Les and I found it hard to comprehend that someone had told this dear little girl at three years of age, "We are your mother and father. You can trust us," and then, after eight or nine months, returned her to an Ontario Children's Aid Society foster home where she regressed to diapers and a bottle. In that foster home she was attended to by an older couple who housed several children.

We first met her on neutral territory, a restaurant, with her social worker. Kelly had big brown eyes, tanned complexion, thick, dark hair and a well-compacted and muscular body. We were told that she was, indeed, bright and that her behaviour had regressed after the failed adoption. Kelly's biologidt⁻ mother was part Irish while her father was of black descent. Since no more details of her conception and birth were given to us, we wondered if her biological father was African American, Mexican or even Native American. One thing was clear; we liked her immediately. Her eyes shone, her smile indicated some shyness, while her body moved adventurously. She was talkative and had a well-developed vocabulary. Apparently she decided she liked us, too. Kelly was always full of creative and unusual

Kelly Ann Evoy, aged five, in 1973.

The Morgan household in Toronto, Ontario, March 1972.

ideas. The day she agreed to be our little girl she said, "I'll be your little girl if I can grow my hair long." What a simple request. No problem. She expressed appreciation for that permission and, all her life, has continued to freely express her gratitude. She became a significant part of our family. She was, and is, our first and chosen daughter.

I was a trained Early Childhood Education teacher and felt eager to make a difference in the world by adopting a child needing a good home. I had loved hundreds of children in my seven year career in day care centres, cooperative preschool programs and English as a Second Language projects. Giving birth to children, from my perspective, was only one way to enjoy the pleasures of fostering the development of children. Les and I had few concerns or apprehensions. Our naive perceptions of adopting an older child were eventually tested and painfully transformed.

I delighted in telling Kelly that our home, soon to be hers, looked like a gingerbread house. It was our first home and we were ever so proud of it. I thought it was cute with trim and leaded windows. Years later I learned that she had felt excited and had very much looked forward to eating the sweets on and in her new gingerbread home. Now an adult, Kelly has told me that she actually believed she was going to have sweets to eat from the eavestroughs. As she said, "I felt ripped off." She jokingly asked me why we didn't, at least, stick a candy cane in the mailbox to enhance the illusion. It was an innocent enough enthusiasm on my part, yet a dissatisfying start from her perspective.

My husband Les, an oil company employee, was supportive to me, agreeable, hesitant to create conflict and considered me *the expert* with children. Regrettably, this attitude distanced him from Kelly. A common statement in those days was, "Whatever you think best, dear." Although his agreeableness definitely made adoption of a beautiful, school-aged girl with a traumatic past a non-marital issue, it was a relationship blessing and problem. I often felt alone in major decision-making in areas concerning Kelly. Our imaginings of the future with Kelly were just that, uninformed. In the seventies, adoption agencies did not have educational and support programs for adoptive parents of older children. Consequently, we had little awareness of the complicated dynamics of adopting a child with a disruptive beginning.

Over the fall of that year, Kelly came for visits: an afternoon, then an overnight stay, leading to a weekend sleepover and a final move in on Boxing Day of 1973. Benjamin, an easy, quiet little boy was receptive to the new excitement. From that Christmas day on, Kelly was a whirl of movement; exploring under and over furniture, trees and Tasha, our Burmese cat. Kelly's gentle handling of Tasha was rewarded with a regular, purring bed companion. Her articulation

Kelly and Ben on Boxing Day 1973, the day Kelly joined our family.

and use of words were creative and abundant. Initially, she wet the bed nightly, sucked her thumb while talking, chewed on her hair and nails, sometimes walked with rigid posture and pinched herself if spoken to firmly. I now know that much of this behaviour is similar to people who have Post Traumatic Stress Disorder. Kelly had experienced extreme stress throughout her young life, including moving in with us. We didn't have adequate skills, knowledge or self-esteem to effectively support her emotional needs. We believed many of her nervous habits calmed over the first few months. In retrospect, she developed strategies to hide her distress from us. Children, being vulnerable to the adult in charge, are often incredibly and creatively adaptive to their environment—often to their own detriment.

She required little sleep and her body seldom seemed to require rest. Kelly's spontaneity and high energy level were incredulous. These high speed attributes can be challenging to those who move and vibrate at a different frequency and pace. It got on our nerves and threw many of our accepted routines into chaos. We filled Kelly's room with books and toys and asked that she keep the noise down after she received her bedtime story. We needed our sleep. Some nights we would pick her up from the floor or half on the bed, half on the floor and return her to bed.

Kelly's feelings of fear, sadness, anger and hurt were most often hidden. At home she tended to present herself with a ready smile and quick comebacks from emotional or physical pain. I remember the rare occasion when she would express feeling angry at me. Regrettably, I would hear an inner voice telling me I was a failure as an adoptive mother. Unable to attend to my own needs, I would unravel emotionally, flip into self-condemnation and give an exaggerated and guilty message of "It's all my fault."

Later, in therapy, I learned that my reaction was connected to my experiences of anger acted out in my family of origin. Because of my tendency to self-blame, Kelly only told me about her problems with other people, never her struggle with my emotional swings. Secondly, it increased pressure on her to please me and keep me happy. Thirdly, it was an incentive to create lies to *protect* me from some of her in-the-world escapades. Unfortunately, lies were a trigger for me to lose my temper. I wish I had had the emotional maturity to better listen to and honour her feelings. I also wish that she had had a father who was connected to her enough to provide her with a safe place to talk.

Of course, I nourished and encouraged, as well. I read bedtime stories, bought educational toys, sewed Kelly pretty dresses, provided lots of creative materials such as crayons, paint, play dough and planned pleasant family meals and outings. She was bright and I would point out her capabilities. She learned, with little coaching, to speed read at a young age. She demonstrated artistic potential and quickly learned facts. She had a charming, fun and enthusiastic personality. Most of all, I did and do love Kelly. I enjoyed cuddling with her and stroking her hair. Along with the moments of me *losing it* we had tender and loving times.

Kelly needed a place to unleash her stress. In grade one, problems began to surface. She did not trust us to hear about her mistakes. With little impulse control she would help herself to things she wanted and had various mishaps outside of the home—mostly at school and at neighbours' homes. Her teachers would describe her as disruptive in the classroom, vying for attention and focusing little on her work. Report cards repeatedly stated "inappropriate attention seeking" and "out of control, impulsive behaviour." I tended to take this feedback as a sign of my personal failure as a parent. Initiated by the educational system's expressed concerns and complaints, we began a long history of accessing community family support services. I needed help with understanding my feelings of anger and powerlessness. I wanted help to learn how to manage Kelly's unpredictable behaviour and repeated school expulsions. Les continued to stay on the sidelines, giving me leadership in parenting matters. While he willingly minded the children during my absences to meetings or courses, his involvement was often diminished out of choice or frequent business travel.

There was a looming worry that perhaps today or tomorrow something nasty would happen. On many days, I believed that all was well and then the phone would ring. Kelly's behaviour was spontaneous and unpredictable. During some more stressful periods with Kelly, I would have bouts of depression, nervousness and moments of irrational anger. My reaction to community disapproval was embarrassment and frustration. When I was unprepared for dealing with the larger system of neighbours and community I felt small and vulnerable.

Underneath my irritated *mother yelling* was a sense of utter helplessness. Eventually I learned that, under my helpless panic was the haunting of my own father's angry outbursts and my mother's complementary posture of powerlessness. From a rough childhood, including a belt whipping rural school master, to serving in the Second World War in the Irish Regiment, where many of his friends were killed, my Dad was a man who never had the opportunity to heal his wounds. I remember a father who was outgoing in nature and worked hard on the farm, but walked rigidly and could not tolerate disagreements or anything less than immediate obedience from me or my three brothers. Among his physical lashing outs was an incident where he discovered me with my playmates on a neighbour's forbidden swing. One minute I was cheerfully on the swing and the next felt my Dad's work boot propel me into the air. Landing on the ground, I didn't yell or scream but followed his order to, "Get home where you belong." For years I walked with a holding pattern in my hip, not knowing why sometimes friends would ask if I was limping. Only in body-focused therapy, several years ago, did my hip release, allowing me to walk with more grace and swing. It is a pleasure now to feel the sway of feminine weight and shape shift from left to right and back again.

On occasion, when I felt out of control with Kelly, Dad's adult temper tantrums and subsequent painful family patterns were relived by me. Although I had made statements such as "I'll never treat my children in an abusive manner," there were times, particularly if I was tired, that I felt triggered, as if a demon had taken over my faculties. From an empty, dark and frenzied place deep in my body, came words and an exasperated hand toward Kelly, who was doing her best in this new family, school and world.

The first incident I remember was about a year after Kelly moved in with us. It was a stormy, icy, winter day as I looked out the living room window and saw Kelly coming home from school. She jumped in front of a car, wiggled her fingers playfully

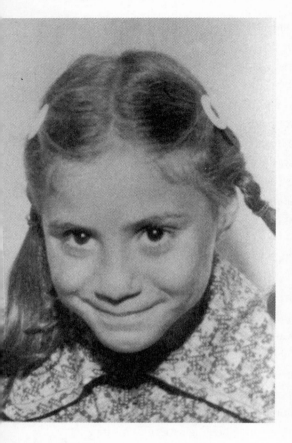

Kelly, aged seven in 1975.

in her ears and made a face at the driver as he frantically swerved his vehicle up onto the side walk. I remember flipping into feelings of absolute panic, fear and outrage. I ran outside, dragged her into the house, threw my car keys at her, began hitting her, and screaming things like, "Who do you think you are? What are you doing—trying to kill yourself?" Then an echo of my father laughed in my ear, "And you thought you could be a better parent than me!" "I am a crazy woman," was my conclusion. That week, I quit my instructing job at Lambton College, began some deep soul searching, and solicited professional guidance and support for Kelly and, particularly, for me, from the Sarnia Lambton Centre for Children and Youth in Sarnia. Les and I attended parenting classes, I joined a Gestalt group for mothers and Kelly was involved in her own therapeutic program. New doors of understanding and support were being opened.

This encouraging arrangement did not last. I had mixed emotions when Les received a training assignment in England from September to April. Initially, I thought the experience in England would be exciting and adventurous. If only I had known what an extrovert I was and how important healthy supports were to me. The winter was long, grey and lonely and I had no friends or family nearby. Les was away a lot and working very hard. I discovered that my birth control had failed us and I was pregnant. Oscillating between feelings of depression and feelings of anger became my norm. Both home life and school were disastrous for Kelly in England. After a particularly frustrating interview with her teacher where I was told, "Kelly should be put in a school for delinquents," I returned home and lost it. I physically attacked her. Kelly now has one word for her memories of our time in England—"nasty." I came back to Canada quite pregnant and, where there was space, was filled with shame.

Feelings of regret over my aggressive reactions motivated me to ask some soul searching questions. I decided that my skills and knowledge were not enough. I needed to look deep inside myself, forgive myself, heal and better manage my behaviours. I committed myself to personal therapy that eventually helped me resolve many of the anxieties rooted in my past family story and failures with Kelly. I no longer hold myself responsible as the guilty party for all of Kelly's unresolved issues. I do, however, take responsibility for the abusive words and actions I directed at her, adding to her baggage of pain. I acknowledge not knowing then, when she first came to us, what I know now. Now, not only do I better understand Kelly's attention

Ben and Kelly in London, England in 1977.

difficulties, I am aware of the dynamics of anger, abuse and abandonment. In moments when I abandoned myself, I was most vulnerable to letting myself and her down.

Entering therapy does not necessarily mean all will be well. It marks the beginning of accepting responsibility for behaviour and a commitment to creating changes. Repeatedly, I had behaviour relapses. I remember thinking I had taken Kelly's hand to escort her upstairs calmly for a time out in her room, rather than yell at her. I felt such discouragement and self-hatred when I discovered my finger prints in her wrist; pink, close to purple, dents. I felt horrified! Doubling my confusion was the fact that I never reacted in aggressive outbursts with Ben. He moved and spoke in gentle, quiet and sometimes humorous ways. I hated the fact that Kelly repeatedly became a target for me. I would internally beat myself up and become emotionally unavailable to her, afraid I would hurt her again. Kelly has since told me that those times when I distanced myself were the scariest for her. Of course, her biggest fear as an adopted little girl, was to be abandoned, yet again. Les continued to be emotionally distant from Kelly. Occasionally he became involved, perhaps containing her with his hands gripped on her shoulders while expressing frustration over some incident. I could easily listen to Kelly's distress over her ensuing hurt and neglected feelings with her Dad.

Ben, Patricia — pregnant with Katie — and Kelly in 1977.

### Morgan Baby

I said to Ben at home one day,
The baby is coming, hip-hurray
I want a girl; Ben wants a boy.
When it comes we'll be full of joy.
Today it is now here.
It is a girl, which is clear.
Hope you are happy, too.

*Kelly Morgan*

A couple of months after Kelly turned nine years old, Katie was born. Kelly and Ben were excited at the prospect of having a baby in the family. Kelly's creative juices flowed when the little baby girl arrived. Katie's birth announcement was made by Kelly (see sidebar).

Kelly now says that, under the circumstances, it was amazing that she did no harm to Katie. She could have had very strong and potentially harmful jealous feelings toward Katie but she did not. Kelly longed to be, and would have benefited from being, the baby of a family. Older, adopted children typically require extra attention and conscious care to establish bonding and trust. Additionally, studies of birth order describe the over responsibility that is often placed on the first born. Parents naturally want a good role model for younger siblings. By the time the youngest child is born, many parents have been educated by the older child (Renee), are more relaxed with eased expectations and have additional assistance to care for the newborn.

Miraculously, Kelly embraced her little sister with excitement, love and enthusiasm. She was a constant source of play, funny faces, amusement and adventure for little Katie. Kelly assisted with diaper changing and feeding. She would rush home from school to spend time with the baby. Our family, at that point, seemed quite settled and normalized. I was receiving excellent support, was glad to be home in Canada and was attending individual and group counselling. Les was more readily available and we joined the Sarnia Riding Club, a family recreational centre on the lake, to ease the pressure on

Les, Patricia, Kelly, Katie and Ben in a family photograph, 1978.

me of managing three children over the summer. Kelly was a terrific swimmer and became a member of the swimming team. She even taught me to do a basic doggie paddle. Ben was happy puddling around with friends and I felt happy to sit under a shade umbrella with the baby. Les joined us for dinner picnics on the beach. Life was better that summer.

Regardless of Kelly's intelligence, attending regular elementary school was becoming more and more restrictive. Repeatedly, teachers complained that she took more time to handle than they had available. Helping professionals in agencies and the local school board recommended we arrange for her to be accepted in a residential children's mental health treatment centre. This was one of the most difficult decisions we had to make as a family. We reasoned that she had experienced too much rejection and abandonment in her life already. After ruling out home schooling, we decided Kelly would live at a children's residential school from Monday to Friday, for a year. Each weekend she came home. That particular year was painful for all of us. I had started university part-time, worked part-time, had a newborn baby, a six year old and a nine year old in a treatment centre. Weekly, we drove an hour and a half, often with the baby breast-feeding on the way, to attend family sessions. The staff at this agency had an invasive attitude and monitored our family life in detail. None of us was the way we were supposed to be, particularly Les and me. I was asked how and why Les had been put on a pedestal in the family. We, for the first time, experienced being blamed; we certainly were not supported.

At one session, after I was told in what ways I had erred with Kelly that week, I started to cry. The next week these so-called professionals declared that they had been too soft on me and had let me control the previous sessions with my crying. They informed Les and me that they were no longer going to be trapped by my game and hold back on what they needed to tell me. I was handed two sheets of paper. One had a list of Pat's Positive Qualities while the other listed Pat's Negative Qualities. Their judging descriptors of me included: manipulative, controlling, can be cruel and negative, dumps energetically on Kelly and blocks change. I cried again. Years later I learned what bruises this agency left in Kelly's history. Punishments at the group home were administered in the name of *behaviour management*. The worst incident was when a sick Kelly was forced to stand in a corner for a long period of time and not be allowed to move, even though she needed to use a toilet. She ended up standing in her own urine and vomit until her time was up and then instructed to clean it up. At nine years of age!

We were directed to continue the program's *consequences*, which were more like punishments. One consequence was called "insight grounding." Kelly was to be in the sight of an adult at all times. On many weekends she slept in our bedroom on a mattress by my side of the bed and was instructed to wake us to go to the washroom. Between nursing Katie in the night and getting up for Kelly, Les and I lost a fair bit of sleep on those weekends. In retrospect, I believe our whole family was injured by these staff members' attitudes and *treatment* methods. I looked elsewhere for my support. My steadfast friend, Mabel, said, "Don't let them abuse you like that," while my Mother said, "They have no idea what it is like to be in your shoes. From what you tell me some of them do not live with children themselves. Can't you laugh at this so called help?" No. I could not. I believed they knew what was best for Kelly and our family. I felt a failure and Les took the lead from me in matters of parenting. We wanted help.

One weekend Kelly lost her new winter coat on the train coming home. The staff instructed Kelly to earn money by washing walls and then took her to a Goodwill thrift store to choose a used coat. Losing things was familiar to us. Kelly had lost a lot of property, very often things she seemed to really value. She began to be sent home in ragged clothes. Two sets of clothing were set aside and she rinsed one set at night before going to bed. Kelly was a sad sight when she came home on weekends, so much so that our neighbours sent us a bundle of clothes for her. I felt a rush of embarrassment when I explained that we could not accept them.

She spent hours being parked on a chair, sleeping on the living room floor rather than in her bedroom, had privileges such as television and allowance withdrawn and was driven to the school each day instead of taking the city bus because of her insight grounding. One week she came home on further restrictions. She was not to watch any television, have no between meal snacks, have no play time, games or extra attention with adults and have an early bedtime. Oh, our dear Kelly! I wanted to believe that eventually all these efforts, restrictions, and disciplines, that felt more like punishments, would make a positive difference.

Many of these stipulations obviously complicated our life, increasing family tension. Though Kelly's life seemed severe we trusted that they knew better than we. Years later when Kelly told me how hard that fourteen months was on her, I had a profound sense of regret. I wish for her and us that Les or I had been more knowledgeable and assertive. I had no awareness of giving away my power. At that time in my life I seldom felt like a powerful individual with most adults, especially ones in positions of authority. If only I could have been more honest with myself, others and particularly, Kelly. I wish Les and I had been sensitive enough to pick up on the severe techniques used by this agency. I can only wonder now if we had been more personally courageous, would Kelly have been spared additional and unnecessary pain?

After her time at this group home was complete, Kelly returned home and we felt some relief. We had a few months of calm and her eleventh summer seemed easier. She played tennis and swam at the Riding Club. Her attentions around baby Katie were committed and intense. She passionately loved the baby and put much energy into giving Katie the kind of infant, toddler and preschool years of which she had been deprived. "Don't make her pick up her toys. I'll do it for her," was a common offer.

### 178 Cecil Street

If you come to our house when Christmas is near,
The socks will be hung before Santa appears.
Mom will be changed after scrubbing the floor.
Dad will be napping with an extra big snore.
Kelly, the gymnast, stands on her head,
While Katie smears jelly on Benjamin's bed.
We sing Christmas carols and sit by the fire.
Candy is out because of our braces.
Still, joy of the season will show on our faces.
We think of you all at this time of year,
Wish you were at our house when Christmas is near.

*Kelly Morgan*

Each Christmas, Kelly's energies tended to be more focused and creative. As a family, we created and enjoyed wonderful celebrations. Kelly enjoyed the treats, the surprises, the preparation, the excitement and was known to find the hidden Christmas presents no matter how clever the secret spot. Once she secretly managed to open a gift of clothing, wear it to school and had it re-wrapped before Christmas Eve. It was so hard for her to wait; as if she was going to explode with the apprehension of pleasure. Her rhyming capability was appreciated and we used her ditties to provide a creative touch to our yearly, home crafted greeting cards.

For ten years we housed, fed and clothed Kelly and continued to follow through on what seemed like logical consequences. As she became older, however, her behaviours became even less manageable. We were not discerning enough to imagine what was going on for her. We sought out a variety of professional help. I received and grew through extensive therapy. Les and I participated in marital and family therapy. Kelly was repeatedly in group counselling programs and therapeutic camps. Often her participation was limited because "she is disruptive to the group" or it was a temporary arrangement; however, it gave us a resting break. Kelly's participation in one hospital-sponsored therapy group for girls was curtailed when I was asked to meet with the supervising psychologist who ended the conversation with, "Has anyone diagnosed your daughter as a sociopath?" What a frightening question to lay before a parent. Thank heavens Kelly wasn't present to hear her conclusion. I felt some fear hearing that "s" word. I was left to research the meaning of this label myself. I knew that Kelly had a *difficult time learning from consequences*, that she was *impulsive* and had a *low tolerance for frustration*. However, the part in the psychology text about being *unable to feel guilt* was not my experience of her. I really sensed that she was struggling internally and had no intention to cause disruption to her world.

For a number of years Kelly enjoyed gymnastics. After taking classes at the YMCA she auditioned and was accepted on a local competitive team. Excitement was in her face each day of her training. I was amazed that she would come home after the roundtrip bike ride on top of the training, and still move in high gear. Unfortunately, due to her impulsiveness, the group situation did not work out for her. It was difficult for me to tell her it was

Kelly demonstrates her gymnastic talents, 1980.

over. Gymnastics had been a logical fit for her inherent need for physical activity. Not only was her body muscular, lithe and graceful, she thrived when moving. I felt heavy and guilty asking myself if Les and I had let professional opinion, once again, sway our decision.

Kelly had a great sense of loss around the gymnastics. She had a strong potential for the sport yet she struggled intensely to contain, listen and follow directions. Internally, she started to view herself as a loser and a failure. I regret that neither Les nor I understood the depth of her loss and discouragement until long after the fact. Her face began to show fewer moments of relaxed happiness and her impulsive behaviours seemed to escalate.

The police would bring her home periodically for strange and impulsive behaviour. On her way to school she and a neighbourhood boy threw garbage cans into the street to watch the traffic become frenzied. At another time, Kelly was walking somewhere, saw a bicycle and had the urge to throw it into traffic to see what would happen. When I asked, "What was going on for you?" her answer was, "You weren't there to say 'no.'" I felt frustrated, trapped and baffled by what was going on for her.

I repeatedly discovered Ben and Kelly stealing and sneaking money out of the house, sometimes in Ben's socks or pockets. After indulging at the local variety store, they would take their candies to school. Report cards commented about Kelly noisily chewing on excessive amounts of candy and gum during school hours. Kelly seemed to have an insatiable desire for sweets. Bags of marshmallows, chocolate chips and other baking items would disappear. Often, desserts would be partially or wholly eaten before they made it to the dinner table. This drive for sweets made no sense to us. Yet, what all of us were not consciously aware of, was the deep despair that existed in Kelly, who shed the odd tear and came back to a hidden and smiling presentation. None of us knew then that she was challenged by a chemical and brain imbalance. So much more is known now about conditions ranging from attention difficulties, brain chemistry, fetal alcohol syndrome, to hereditary factors and the effects of deficient infant bonding.

When Kelly lied, she was trying to protect us from behaviour she regretted and could not explain. So much energy was spent by Kelly in image management. Think about the vigor it takes for professional models to present themselves in a certain manner. Here was a child exerting herself to keep herself safe from, I am sad to say, her father and me. The mistakes were big in her eyes and, in a bizarre way, she was looking after her caregivers. No decent job for any child.

Watching her interact with Katie was still a delight for me. She fussed and nurtured Katie whenever she could. She began to coach Katie in gymnastic moves and would include other younger neighbour children in the activity. Suzy, a little girl from Jamaica, moved in next door and became Katie's playmate. Kelly fell in love with Suzy and would be seen in the front garden on her back trying to balance the two of them on her feet. She was also a willing helper in the kitchen, seeming to genuinely enjoy tackling tasks with me. Chris, a sweet and quiet girl, became Kelly's best friend. Years later I heard about the troubling behaviour in which Chris and Kelly engaged.

In grade eight, Kelly's teacher complained about her lack of completed homework, tension with classmates and eating excessive amounts of candy and junk food. At our first parent-teacher interview, this teacher asked Les and me if we had considered seeking professional help. This time I asserted myself. "I feel stunned by your question. Have you not read her records?" Kelly was periodically suspended from class that year. It meant I had to supervise her at home. More tension.

Kelly's acting out behaviours increased in her thirteenth year. Running away began and police involvement increased. At this stage in her life, she had basically given up all hope of succeeding in our family. This giving up had many consequences as will be further revealed in later chapters. It is regrettable that at a time in our life when we were beginning to have better coping skills, Kelly had given up on us...and herself. Tension and troubles escalated.

We arranged for a private counsellor to see Kelly every second week with the rationale that, having an additional, but neutral, person to keep an eye on her and connect with her, would be helpful. For several months she also went by train to London to see one of her previous group home workers who was now studying art therapy. We also arranged for her to attend a wilderness school, Outward Bound, hoping that would make a difference. Kelly seemed to appreciate and look forward to all three of these experiences.

To solve the babysitting problem, we advertised at the Community College for a live-in student to help with child care and household tasks. Luanne lived with us from Monday to Friday for two years, making it possible for me to attend university classes and not rely totally on Les to be home. Cooking for six people was not something I particularly enjoyed, but the payoffs with Luanne living with us were wonderful. I learned that the more supports I put in place, the less I lost my temper and composure with the stresses of a busy family life and Kelly's unpredictable behaviours. Also, focusing on my own goals and studies gave me a sense of being in control of my life.

We did require other services on the weekends for care. One weekend, Les and I went away for an overnight trip. We hired an older lady who was known in Sarnia by many doctors and more affluent families as a solid caregiver. When we returned the woman told us this story. "I realized about one o'clock in the morning that Kelly wasn't here. I prayed for an hour or so for her to return. Then your Benjamin came downstairs and said, 'Don't worry. It's not your fault. My sister runs away sometimes.' Because of that incident, the next time we took an overnight break we hired a young married couple. On our return they reported that Kelly had been driving our car, had moved several teenagers into the house and some of our property had been stolen. Repeatedly, we felt trapped in an untenable situation. I understand now that Kelly had found acceptance among peers where her adventurous and spontaneous nature was celebrated. Grounded parent-child relationships are developed from birth through the elementary school years. With a solid foundation or safety net, teens can explore who they are, what values they embrace and what behaviours are a fit for them. The net we had provided for Kelly was fragile and unreliable.

Around this time in our life, Les' mother died and Peter, his mentally challenged brother, came to live with us. We eventually arranged for him to live with a couple who provided room and board. We continued to be the main supervisors of his care. He came on Sundays for dinner, Wednesdays for his allowance, and he joined us for any special celebrations. Peter enjoyed taking long walks and was known to get lost. Les would sometimes spend late nights out looking for Peter and keeping his eyes open for Kelly. At other times he would be out looking for Kelly and keeping his eyes open for Peter. We had no way to know how eager Kelly was to really leave home, or to know how deep her pain was in remaining at home and attempting to attend school.

With each teen year, the chaos escalated. Photographs of Kelly became sparse in our albums. She repeatedly ran off, had shoplifted, skipped school and experienced several expulsions from high school. By the age of sixteen she only had five secondary credits, despite her ability to speed read and creatively write prose and poetry. In later years I learned that she began a drug habit at the age of thirteen years. At that time I was attempting to stop her from smoking cigarettes. I would drown the cigarette packages in the kitchen sink any time I found them in the house. How naive I was. Yet I cared dearly.

Les and I wanted a miraculous change to calm our struggles with Kelly. We, and I in particular, really believed there was some magical formula to discover. I clung on to the idea that if I just read the right book, found the right therapist for me or her or all of us, or never, never lost my temper again or said "I love you" in a better way, that all would be well. The fact was that high school was like hell for Kelly and none of us clued in to the emotional and neurological reasons.

After Kelly's first high school expulsion I spent hours on the phone negotiating with the school board to find another school for Kelly. A second high school agreed to accept her but, after a couple of months, Les and I were asked to meet with them. The principle informed us that her behaviour was impacting other students' learning. The science teacher, who was a bundle of nerves, said that they had been studying friction with blocks and resistance. Kelly had played with these objects rather than do the assignment. The teacher expressed fear because the next week the class was going to work with Bunsen burners. Kelly was asked to leave her second high school. Again I was on the phone to the school board. This time the officials agreed to accept Kelly into Sarnia's only alternative high school for challenging teenagers. On some days, half the class was absent, often in jail. Then Kelly became involved with the juvenile court system over shoplifting. Generous Christmas gifts from Kelly turned out to be stolen property. Again, her inability to plan, wait and comprehend the consequences of her behaviour showed itself. Her immediate desire was to please us with wonderful gifts. I smile now at the thought of her attempt...but that Christmas I was not in light and joy.

We had a court assessment that stated that Les was to provide more one-to-one positive time with Kelly while I was to increase my letting go of *owning* Kelly's behaviour problems. Ordering a father to become more involved and a mother less involved without any suggestion of how is an unrealistic directive. There were many past and present dynamics to support us in our respective commitments. Les was not bonded to Kelly and to this day tends to be a non initiator in relationships. They also recommended that we go out more often for couple time. Again, the court did not suggest how we were to make this happen. Based on our experience of arranging hired child care we often felt uneasy leaving home for very long.

The police continued to visit us for one reason or other. Either Kelly was on the street with an open beer bottle or she had committed another minor but troubling behaviour. Six year old Katie would answer the door and, as casually as if she were announcing a neighbour was there to borrow sugar, she would say, "There's a policeman to see you, Mom."

Then there were the spooky, late night happenings. The phone rang and a young man's voice said, "Is Kelly there?" After I said, "No, she is asleep," he spoke in an offensive manner to me. On another night a car drove over the sidewalk and up onto our front lawn with a carload of young guys yelling profanities. Sometimes our dog, Sissy, began barking and in the wee morning hours in our back garden would be a gang of young people *partying*. Kelly never used language with us like these invaders. We were unaware of just how involved Kelly was in a subculture of Sarnia of which we had no experience, let alone knowledge: the drug scene. The little of Kelly we knew began to slip away as she felt a better sense of belonging with her peers.

When Kelly turned fifteen years old, I began studying for a master's degree. Ben was twelve years old and eager to look after Katie who was then six. He walked her to school, looked after her at lunchtime and watched over her until Les or I was home by late afternoon. It did seem time for me to separate from Kelly's troubling behaviours. Having classmates and a purpose outside of parenting and homemaking was really a self-supportive move on my part. The Centre for Humanistic Studies in Detroit became a haven for me that year. I drove an hour and a half, to and from Detroit, three times a week to this most nurturing, academic institution. Professors hugged students as they entered class and I felt my best qualities begin to blossom. It was here that the full idea of "it is your life Patricia that you control" became clear for me. The rest, including Kelly, was not in my power and control. By giving up illusions of power and control over her, my feelings of frustration minimized and I felt internally stronger.

During my studies, I began to explore my past experiences through journal recording and prose. I searched for meaning to my experiences as a stretched mother and developed a new appreciation for the efforts and struggles of my own father.

## Farmer's Daughter

I see the burdened shoulders of my father.
He fights the earth; he spits the dust.
He plants the seeds and prays.
The rain wins his gratitude or hate.
While his angry fist cries for survival
His muscular, weather beaten body
Is propelled outdoors to God's given day.
My childhood memory has me small
Under the presence of my father.
He loomed so mighty—
For he had faced terror;
The war, the bull, the blood he shed.
The fear of a crop unripe
Frightened supreme.
The safety and feeding
Of his family always
In the mind of my father
As he proclaimed determination
To heaven above.

*Patricia Morgan*

The year Kelly turned sixteen, I completed a master's degree. I had spent hours and days studying, reading books and taking psychology courses to find out the answers to help change Kelly's chaotic and impulsive behaviours. I had attended Mommy therapy, parenting groups, group therapy, personal therapy, couple therapy and family therapy with mixed successes. My reactions were calmer with fewer and fewer moments of feeling out of control. Our marriage changed. Les and I knew ourselves and each other better. I felt sorrow that Kelly experienced me as a safe and caring mother, only in rare moments.

Despite all we had been through, Kelly's last and final school expulsion came as a shock to me. The notification of suspension read, "Conduct injurious to moral tone of school. Kelly is habitually late. Kelly does not work well during work periods. Kelly frequently disturbs students around her." Again I was negotiating with the school board. I was expected in classes myself and found it disheartening and irksome either to have Kelly home alone or to have to miss classes to be home with her. It was agreed that Kelly, on Mondays to Fridays, would receive an hour of one-on-one teaching at the board office. I would drop her off and wave to her as she went into the building. She used a bus to get home. After about three weeks I received a phone call from the board of education saying that they had not seen Kelly, ever. Not once had she attended her tutoring. I was asked, "Wasn't this the agreement?"

No matter all the therapy, all the support I had put in place and the long period I had remained feeling whole and steady, at that moment I lost myself. I went looking for her and found her at a local mall smoking with a group of young people. I caused a loud scene in front of her friends. What to do next?

Back to the drawing board! Les and I were beside ourselves. We offered to pay first and last month's rent on an apartment, to buy pots and pans, to provide setting-up-home stuff and help her get a job somewhere, like working in a donut shop. I encouraged, "You could satisfy your sweet tooth." We were feeling desperate. She said she did not want to leave home, did not want to work but wanted to continue in school. I wanted to believe her, to be on her side and to be her cheerleader. Once again, I was on the phone to the school board. This time they agreed that Kelly could return to the regular school system after she either held down a job for six months or acquired a summer school credit. Kelly chose earning a summer school credit. She turned sixteen years of age, attended summer school for less than a week, and then disappeared.

We had no idea Kelly was deeply involved with drugs and was struggling to keep a toe in our home. From age thirteen on, she had slipped further and further away from us, and in many ways, from herself. It was the beginning of addiction's abduction that really escalated on that summer day, when Kelly exited our family life.

In some ways I had prepared myself for her leaving. I sensed that we could not tolerate her increasingly dark side and that she would soon bolt from the restrictions we placed on her. We attempted to keep some sense of family saneness for ourselves and our other two children. When I consider how distant she felt from herself and us, and how involved she was with drugs, it is impressive that she slugged out those disastrous adolescent years at home waiting until she was sixteen to leave. She left in the middle of the night, with another teen well known to the police, when Les was away on a business trip. It felt final because I found a goodbye note on the dining room table. The note speaks of love and sorrow.

*Mom,*
*Sorry I didn't give you a month's notice, but I have to leave. I hate not being trusted and I knew you were hurt by my lie yesterday. I will get a hold of you to get the rest of my clothes etc. I love you and I'm sorry it's ending like this.*

*Love, Kelly*

After reading her note I felt loss, sadness and an element of emergency. In the morning I called the Children's Aid Society, the Sarnia Police and our lawyer. The police recommended that the house locks be changed. They recognized the name of Kelly's friend saying, "That teen is known for break and enters." That afternoon a locksmith came to secure the house. Locking Kelly out seemed so contradictory to spending all those years trying to get our family life straightened away so that we could really embrace her. Though the door was locked, my heart was not.

Les was still away, and I realized that many incidents happened when Les was away. I again felt emotionally alone in my grief and care. Fortunately, I had learned some coping mechanisms so I phoned my friends, Mabel and Margaret and my mother for support and comfort. That morning I thought of nothing but Kelly, worried about her and had a distressing image. I saw myself one day, not so far away, visiting her in jail.

# 2
# ...from a distance

GRIEVING HAD TO BE DONE. Letting go is not easy for me. I experienced a pull-push either to continue to distance from Kelly or to figure out how to maintain some kind of connection to her. That first summer we saw her four or five times. I longed to say, "Please come home." Yet I had a sense that she needed to take her life in another direction, away from us, before she would be ready for a turn around. I had no clue how long that other direction would be or how deeply into crime and drugs it would take her.

A week after she left, Kelly rang the door bell saying, "I'd like my clothes and can I have my teddy bear and my roach clips?" After Ben and I brought her items to the front door, her male companion said, "Shit, Kelly. We can't hit the highway with all this." A couple of weeks later she came again to get some more clothes. We said no to taking away her bedroom dresser. Once she came specifically asking for a glass of orange juice. "All we get is coffee," she explained of where she was living with a friend's family.

One night when we all went out for dinner, Ben started saying silly one liners and we laughed. We looked at each other and realized, "We are laughing. There is no tension. It is OK to lighten up and have fun." Our family life from that day on became easier, although there was always the unease of how to protectively, yet caringly, keep connection with Kelly.

By October of 1984, Kelly moved to somewhere outside Kitchener, Ontario. She arranged to come for Christmas and I noticed she had very little to say about her activities or life. She seemed very aloof.

After Christmas she disappeared. That was an agonizing time for me. Every day I wondered where and how she was. The following May I heard that the body of a teenager with dark hair and skin, wearing blue jeans, had been taken out of the St. Clair River and the police were looking for someone who could identify the body. I felt such a rancid sickness in my gut. I did not want to go to the morgue. I began making

Kelly, Katie, Ben and Patricia. Kelly visits at Christmas 1984.

phone calls and leaving messages asking Kelly to call me.

She called from a home for pregnant teenagers asking, "Why do you want to know where I am? What business is it of yours?" I told her my dilemma, "All I ask is to know you are alive and well." She responded to my plea with sobs and seeming relief. A couple of days later she called to ask if I would come to the Kitchener hospital. She was having an operation to abort a hydatiform mole or *false pregnancy*.

While I was by the side of her hospital bed she asked if she could come home. I took some deep breaths. I believed that she sincerely wanted to move home and start fresh, yet, I was not willing to potentially bring chaos back into our home. After discussing the options with Les, I presented an offer to Kelly. I would arrange for her to live at a girls' home in London, called Belton House. She could come home on weekends and, after her first school report card, we would check to see if she was ready to return home. I left her with ample money and my fingers crossed.

After less than three weeks at Belton House, Kelly left and was not welcome back there—something to do with drugs. She disappeared again.

In Canada, until a young person reaches the age of eighteen, parents are informed if they are involved in law breaking. The judicial system provided us with a tracking of Kelly's whereabouts. In October 1985, I made my first visit to a jail to visit Kelly. Booth House was a jail for young women near London. Kelly had been sent there on a drug related charge for three months, to be followed by a year's probation. I felt awkward and distressed. Kelly seemed cut off from me by an invisible, yet very thick, barrier. After my visit, I called to see how she was doing, only to be told she had been sent to a high security facility for fifteen days. By Christmas, Kelly was in another jail, Elgin Middlesex Detention Centre. We were informed that there was no point in taking her gifts as she would not be allowed to have them.

That Christmas seemed quite symbolic for me. She was in jail, not among us opening gifts and sharing in the festivity. Christmas had long been a creative and fun occasion in our family and Kelly had always participated with enthusiasm and imagination. The experience reminded me of mourners' descriptions of the death of a loved one creating "a deep hole on special occasions." This time I really grieved the loss of my daughter as I had known her in Christmases past.

Sometimes Kelly called from someone's home, sometimes from a hospital but most often, it seemed, she called from jail. I soon learned that you cannot make a direct phone call to a jail inmate. You can only leave a message for the individual to call, and if you are lucky, the message gets through. In my case, I was never sure whether or not Kelly would choose to respond. I liked it when she was in jail because I worried less, knew she had a bed and food, and because I had an address to which I could send her a letter. I was committed to, at least, continuing to let her know that I loved her.

In 1987 Les was transferred to Calgary, Alberta. I had such mixed emotions about leaving Sarnia where we had received extraordinary support and encouragement, yet for years I felt uncomfortably visible as a *struggling mother* and *client* to most available helping agencies. I liked the idea of experiencing the possibilities of a new identity in a fresh community. I also wondered about the impact on Kelly. Would this represent ultimate abandonment? I resolved to write letters regularly, mailing them "in care of" her present boyfriend's mother. This boyfriend represented, for us, a deepening of Kelly's illegal activities. Tommy, a former bike gang member, had been recently released from an extensive jail term because of organized drug dealings.

She would call periodically and end the conversation with, "I love you." I was always grateful for that. "Oh, nothing much," was her repeated response to my inquiries of her life. When she told us she was a waitress in a bar, we thought that just did not sound like a good fit for her. Her inability to focus, remember, and carry through would be definite obstacles in that job. About the same time Ben showed us the contents of an envelope he had received from Kelly. It contained pornographic-like photos and a note saying, "Look at these. They're proof I strip. Mail them back before Mom and Dad see them." Little hints of her experiences shot into our very middle class life in Western Canada.

September 1988 Kelly called direct from a doctor's office to announce that she was pregnant with Tommy's baby. My breath froze. I remember saying, "Sounds like a big responsibility for you, dear." I thought. "Oh dear! She is twenty years old and a baby herself in many ways."

Kelly hitchhikes across Canada, seven months pregnant in 1989.

In January 1989 at 6:00 a.m. the phone rang. "I'll be in Calgary tomorrow, Mom. I miss you guys. Please pick me up at the bus station." Les rolled over from his side of the bed to ask, "What's that about?" His response to my answer was to turn on his stomach, pound his pillow and moan, "Shit! Shit! Shit! She will have the baby here and then what?" At the bus terminal the next morning, I did not know whether to laugh, cry or scream. There she stood — broad smile, seven months pregnant, wearing a man's red and black lumber jacket, a pair of dirty, loose fitting men's sneakers and a grubby Mickey Mouse T-shirt. I hugged her.

She told me that she and Tommy were at a London bar when they began to argue. He told her to "fuck off." So she did. She went out to the street, with only a couple of dollars in her purse and put her thumb out to hitch hike. "Calgary, please." Things went quite well until she hit Thunder Bay. After she used a garage washroom, she discovered that her last ride had driven away with her purse, leather jacket and shoes. Someone took pity on her and provided her with the lumber jacket, old runners and a one way bus ticket to Calgary.

Les and I were, initially, nervous about Kelly's visit. Our experience, however, was a pleasing one. She said she wanted to learn to cook, not that we had much success accomplishing that. She just could not seem to focus. Les enjoyed the caring efforts of, "Can I make you a coffee, Dad?" And, "Let me clean that up for you." After several days, however, she was acting agitated, said she was ready to leave and return to Tommy, who by this time had *made up* over the phone. We talked about putting her on a comfortable flight to return to Ontario and decided that paying for the bus travel expense was a reasonable compromise.

When she left, I had renewed hope that an innocent baby would bring a sense of responsibility and stimulate some change for Kelly. At a minimum, we felt a fresh and soft connection to her, not having to be so guarded. James Eric was born March 7, 1989 in London, Ontario.

That spring we sent money for first and last month's rent and I made a trip to Ontario to see the new baby. They were a young family living on welfare in a tiny basement apartment with pipes overhead and a water leak above their arborite kitchen table. It was like visiting many young families — the smell of diapers, lack of sleep, and pride in the new little one. In my arms I held a perfect form of human life and felt a strange blessedness in accepting the title "Grandma."

Les had business trips to Ontario and would try to see Kelly, especially since she now had a steady address. He would take gifts and greetings. The young family decided to move into an apartment building owned by Lillian, Tommy's mother. Lillian provided many services, including baby care, to the new family while we financially helped with first and last month's rent. We also funded a visit to Calgary for baby Jamie and Kelly. The visit was a pleasant one. Later we found out that Kelly was pregnant and Danielle was born December 11, 1990. From our perspective, Kelly's life looked calmed. How well she deceived us.

I tried to get to Ontario twice a year to see my own mother and drop in on Kelly and her family. After one visit Lillian called Calgary in a panic asking me, "Please do something." Kelly, she said, was leaving for days at a time, getting drunk and had recently come home hysterical with a needle stuck in her arm. Apparently the needle had broken off and she had refused to go to a doctor. I called Kelly that night and she confirmed everything and added, "They won't let me go to school and I hate being on welfare. I wish you were closer. It's awful after you leave." She told me that she would stop drinking and using drugs a couple of days before our arrival. Each time we came she would get herself into a sober state. Kelly's truth and depth of addiction were becoming clearer, as was the importance of us in her life. I resolved to call her and write more often.

Soon after that, Kelly left Tommy, moved into a flat and began single parenting. She was initially more available for phone conversations and then, after she mentioned a new boyfriend, I could not connect with her for months.

In the summer of 1992 Les was transferred to Ontario and we moved to an older, in-need-of-renovation house in Burlington. I was pleased to be nearer my mother, other relatives, old friends and, of course, Kelly and her children. I created images of a cookie baking grandma like the ones on the television commercials. Kelly, however,

Les, Katie, Ben, Jamie, Kelly and Patricia. Kelly visits with baby Jamie in 1990.

was living in another world — high or drunk and very difficult to engage in conversation. She certainly was not available for the Sunday dinner visits I wanted to arrange. This was very disheartening now that we were living a two hour drive away, rather than across the country.

She phoned a couple of weeks before Christmas saying she wanted to spend the holidays with us. It was arranged. She seemed on edge for those couple of days, ate frequently from the fridge, slept at erratic hours, had the children wrapped in her arms like love bugs or was yelling at them for incidentals. We knew little about addictions and could not tell if she was using drugs while with us or was in some kind of withdrawal state.

A couple of months later in 1993, Kelly was evicted from her flat. She was living partly in a women's half way house and partly with a girlfriend while the children slept, most days, at Lillian's place. Kelly's addictions were becoming obvious. She convinced me that she could stop if she just left London and started a new life. Three times I arranged to pick her and the children up in London and take them to Martha House, a women's interval home near Burlington. The first two times I phoned before leaving to check if she was ready. Twice she went out *partying* the night before my expected arrival to celebrate her leaving, had lost all her money and was hung over. On the third agreed upon date I decided to make the trip to London, regardless.

That day in March I arrived at a pigsty of a house. I made my way past littered beer bottles, flooded ashtrays, an unplugged refrigerator with visible molding food, and holes punched in various walls, to a room piled with dirty clothes and a mattress. In front of me was my beautiful Kelly — sweaty, drawn face, anorexic looking with track marks up her arms, passed out in the middle of this filthy rumple. When she looked up at me, I saw a little, lost girl... and then she smiled and said, "Hi, Mom." All I could say was, "Let me get you out of here, dear."

We picked up the children. I brought all three to Burlington and then to the women's shelter. Things went smoothly for a couple of weeks. I took Kelly and the children for a daily outing; she said she was looking into housing at other times in the day. Our home was undergoing internal construction with a gutted kitchen so I tried to reduce the time the children came over. It was simply unsafe.

Les and I had planned a four day visit back to Calgary. I told Kelly, "I have friends who will visit you and help you continue to settle in the community." She declined the offer. I had an uneasy feeling leaving her while saying to myself, "She is an adult. Live your own life, Patricia. If she wants to create a new life it is best she put out most of the effort."

When I returned to Burlington I learned that Kelly had been evicted from the women's shelter and no one was sure where she was. The Children's Aid Society had become involved and the children were back in London with Tommy and his mother, Lillian.

Les and I were asked by the Children's Aid worker if we would consider taking temporary custody of the children. The situation for the children was not the healthiest with Tommy and Lillian but it was far superior, the worker believed, to living with Kelly in her erratic, addicted state. If we were interested, he thought James and Danielle would be better off with us. For their sake foster homes were to be avoided. I was longing to say, "Yes." Two big "buts" stopped us. Les did not want to begin caring for children again. I certainly would want a supportive partner if I took on this responsibility. The other was, what if getting well for the children's sake was the only motivator Kelly had? If the children lived with us, perhaps she would decide they were really *better off* and continue to sink deeper into her addictions. We declined. To this day I hold great appreciation and gratitude for the children's other grandmother, Lillian. For several years she fed, clothed, nursed and protected them, to the best of her ability, in a small two bedroom apartment, receiving periodic and small bits of financial help from us.

Kelly became *a person with no fixed address*, living in a multitude of places in London. She visited the children; I do not know how often depending on the depth of her addictions and whether she was in hospital or jail. I began to write frequently "in care of Lillian," the children's other grandmother.

In April 1993 Kelly called me from a London hospital in need of financial assistance to purchase a body brace. She was at risk of becoming confined to a wheel chair. Kelly and a friend had rolled a stolen taxi and she had multiple injuries including a cracked vertebra. Plans were put in place to have a brace made for her and I called the hospital to arrange the necessary payment, only to be told she had left the hospital that night. Over and over, Kelly seemed to be committing a slow suicide. The mother in me wanted to SCREAM! I felt so powerless. That was the morning I decided to post only photocopied letters, letters that might, one day, help someone else struggling with a similar situation. How do you successfully love an addicted loved one?

# 3
## ...the letters

T O THE READER: IN THE FOLLOWING THIRTY LETTERS to Kelly I now see that a number of the initial messages, I wrote with emotional manipulation. In the May 30, 1993 message, in particular, I see an attempt to lay a guilt trip. However, writing letters not only allowed me to keep contact with Kelly, but provided a means for me to observe my own thinking and communication. As a long time journaller, I know the power of writing; you experience yourself in black and white.

By 1995 my letters began to have clearer messages of acceptance, encouragement and unconditional love. Change is possible; I changed and, if you have the desire, so can you. May you find some insight for your situation reflected in my attempts to maintain some kind of relationship with Kelly, my addicted loved one.

April 16, 1993
Burlington, Ontario

Oh dear Kelly!

I called Victoria Hospital this morning to arrange for the body brace. I was told that you walked out of the hospital last night. A nurse told me that a brace had been made for you, was delivered this morning and they sent it away because your whereabouts were unknown.

Of course, I am stewing about your safety, your health, and wondering how guilty to feel—a mother thing. Did you give up? Leave the hospital because of something I said to you, or did not say on the phone yesterday? Was it because I did something? Mother guilt, that is one of my problems. Maybe you left for some other reason.

Please look after yourself. Apparently you are at risk walking about and **should** have stayed in the hospital longer. You know you could end up paralyzed and confined to a wheel chair.

It is your life. Please take care of it. I am feeling absolutely helpless.

Love, Mom

May 11, 1993
Burlington, Ontario

Dear Kelly

I forget the last time we talked. I expect it was when you were in the hospital and needed a body brace. I did write you a note, horrified that you walked out of the hospital needing that body brace for risk of ending up in a wheel chair, paralyzed.

Since then your Grandpa Ted died and Mother's Day has passed. I asked Les to call Tommy and give him the news of my dad's death. Katie said you called one day and talked to her. So I gather you know about Grandpa.

Ben could not come to Dad's funeral. He phoned and sent a letter. He also went to Edmonton and spent time with Uncle John to grieve. I felt sad, glad and angry—a whole bunch of feelings. In the last few years, I had developed a new appreciation for my dad. I still feel some anger about his abusive moments with me, without ever an apology.

Although I believe I have forgiven him for the wounds he passed on to me I will hold him responsible for his mean behaviours. I trust you to hold me responsible for the times I let you down and hurt you.

I have spent a lot of time in Fenelon Falls with Grandma Mary and she is doing fine, crying sometimes, laughing others. She lived a stressful life with Dad. He sure did have an anger management problem. So did I. Too bad he did not get help to bring him more peace.

So Ben was not at the funeral. Neither were you. I forget what I told people when they asked about you. I have a number of memory losses from that time. More than three hundred people came and went. Katie and Les were there for me. I had no idea how exhausting the death of a parent can be. I read the eulogy, a review of Dad's life including memories, stories and happenings such as his role in freeing Holland during the Second World War. I felt honoured to be chosen to read my father's eulogy with Uncles Jim, John and Paul's support to do so. I have never felt closer to my brothers, Mom, aunts, uncles and cousins. Every one of our cousins came. So many people who have loved and been loved by Grandma Mary came to give her hugs and comforting messages. I felt overwhelmed. What a terrific, adored mother I have.

I was glad to be with her on Mother's Day. Your dad had gone canoeing and Katie was clowning in Hamilton. She gets better and better at twisting balloons into animals and making children smile. Grandma and I talked some about you, caring about you, wondering, "Is Kelly lost to us?" I do not know how to make contact with you Kelly. I feel ineffective in giving you the message of "I love you" and I am sincerely sorry for any harm I may have caused you.

Please take care of yourself and I am here if you want a hug or a listening ear.

With love, Mom

May 16, 1993
Burlington, Ontario

My dear Kelly

  You called this Friday. I wanted to remember some of the things you shared with me because I felt tender while listening. I believe that, maybe for the first time, the inner Kelly, the Kelly who was so badly hurt and abandoned, was speaking to me. I hope I listened with a gentle ear.

  Some things I remember hearing are:

- Ken, an older and kind taxi cab driver, took you in and provides you with room and food.
- You appreciate all he has done for you.
- You have been attending AA meetings.
- You feel frustrated, and perhaps pissed off, with Tommy's misuse of illegal drugs.
- You worry about Danielle and James.
- You love and respect your Dad and wonder if he has given up hope for you getting healthy.
- You have beaten yourself up since you were very little when you made mistakes and you felt so crumby that you would lie to hide the mistakes from us.
- You remember a time when your foster mother lit a cigarette lighter under your fingers when you were reaching for a cookie.
- A worker from the residential home told you that the only reason I wanted to adopt you was to make you into a "perfect" kid so that I could show you off to my friends.
- You wonder sometimes if we, Dad and I, want you when we already have a "perfect" son and a "perfect" daughter. Do you really believe we have two "perfect" children to show off to our friends?
- You feel me distancing myself especially when you are "doing bad." I would say it is more often when you come forward as tough and laughing at me when I express concern. Then I back off.
- You want me to know that when you "act tough" you do not want me to distance myself. That is a hard one for me. I feel scared of tough guys.
- You feel sensitive about our unease at loaning or giving you money.

- You appreciated what Dad and I did when you were at Martha House and you felt like "a burden on us." I am older, wiser and seldom do what I do not want to do from my heart.
- When you used to "screw up" as a kid, you would feel so ashamed after "these people adopted me."
- You are wondering about your biological mother and wondering if some personal questions, you have, would be answered if you met her. Even seeing her would make a difference to you.
- Lying "on the street" is normal and people on the street know you do not mean what you say. You believe I should know that what you say is not necessarily the truth. My experience with you has you getting quite huffy if I challenge what you say.
- If you start to have some successes in your life, you do not want me to show too much excitement. At the same time, you like my support and encouragement and want me to give you credit.
- When you have "blown it" around getting back on to a healthy track you give up and do even more self-destructive behaviours.
- You are starting to fear that early death may be a result if you do not make some changes.
- You know that your death would have a large and negative impact on Danielle and James.
- In the past you pushed yourself fast to get healthy and you faltered.
- This time you are going to be more patient and kind to yourself.
- You are aware that going back to school will not address the emotional issues that keep you from loving yourself. I agree. You would not talk to me about counselling before but you would talk about school.
- You were introduced to inner child or re-parenting counselling when you were in rehabilitation a couple of years ago. You felt uncomfortable with it and cried. I imagine crying feels scary for you and maybe it was just what you needed to do, cry and feel some of your buried pain.
- Boredom has long been a challenge for you. You are smart enough to know that boredom is sometimes used as an excuse not to feel what you are feeling.
- At one time you thought you could get on with life without engaging in counselling. You now believe that sorting out and remembering your childhood is important.

- You remember many of your childhood memories going back to quite a young age. That is an encouraging sign.
- You and I both wonder if some sexual abuse happened in your young years. You remember a boy in your bunk bed at the foster home.
- You feel some jealousy around Ben and Katie. You feel more comfortable with Ben than Katie.
- You have not told me many of the stories that have filled your days after leaving home.
- You are willing to do some work with seniors or others in return for your welfare cheque..
- You find it easier to cry and take risks telling me about your hurt, disappointment and anger over the phone than in person.
- You are in physical pain from the car accident and other assaults to your precious body.
- Thinking about giving up "street life" is scary for you but you feel worried about yourself and your children if you do not choose another lifestyle.
- You wonder why after ten years of living with us, having a middle class lifestyle with food, rules, clothes, books, values, proper grammar, holidays, hugs and attention, you are still struggling so much. You had a very rocky beginning, abandoned so many times by your biological mother and the other family, who said they were adopting you and kept you for only eight months. Then there were foster families and then there was me with my temper outbursts and other neurotic behaviours. You know what other bumps and disappointments you have survived.
- You wonder if it is too late to sort your life out. Never! You deserve to get what you did not get. Others and I can help as you clearly say what you want. Please ask me to lend you Suzanne Summer's book, **Keeping Secrets**. She and others have turned around after years of feeling lost.
- You felt relaxed, real and loved as our conversation continued. You risked telling me who you are and what you have done, thought and believed in the past. I heard you and you were OK and I was OK.

Love you, Mom

May 30, 1993
Burlington, Ontario

My dear Kelly

I felt relieved that you agreed to come here for a rest. We got penicillin for your strep throat Thursday. You were a wonderful help around the house when you felt up to it. I was pleased with your responsible management of the neck brace and penicillin. I enjoy your appreciation and conversations. Please understand Kelly that I felt hurt by HOW you left, not by your leaving and going back to London.

Thank you for calling this morning. I am glad you are safe. Because we love you, your decisions and lifestyle do affect us.

We did not experience you as a burden, neither while you were here with us, nor when you and the children were at Martha House in Hamilton. I find that I feel burdened by your addictions, your "partying," your not keeping your agreements, your unresolved issues that require some committed counselling and your inability to provide a consistent home for Danielle and James. These all burden me; never the decisions that move toward health and well being for you.

I am sure I will hear the story sometime of how you ended up in London last night. From my perspective last week I agreed to drive to London to arrange for a body brace for you and bring you back to Burlington to convalesce. Then last night you went out to watch the hockey game on a big screen and never came home.

You are wearing Katie's black jacket and black stretch pants. She and I do not like that you did not respectfully come home and change out of them before going. I feel abandoned and minimized by being left here with your dirty and clean clothes, medicine, night sleeping brace, throat lozenges, penicillin and a big bowl of your favorite potato salad. Thank heavens you are wearing your body brace—or is that an assumption on my part? I imagine this is how Danielle and James feel. As if, one minute, or day or month Mom is here loving, stroking, laughing, encouraging and then the next, for no understandable reason, she is gone. The difference between me and your children, Kelly, is that I know that this is about you and your addiction trap. But James and Danielle are young, unaware, naive children, who like most children will probably decide that the reason you are not there consistently with planned separations is because they are not good or loveable enough.

When you violate agreements, we become more cautious. You are welcome and loved here. Please come when you realize that it is a wise thing for you to do and please leave in a more considerate manner.

As I am off to paint the woodwork in the family room I am muttering, "The story is not over."


Love, Mom

July 5, 1993
Burlington, Ontario

My dear Kelly

Where did the month go? At the end of May you were here. June 17 was the first I heard anything and that was from a nurse at Victoria Hospital informing me of your stab wound. Kelly, I called the hospital to see about coming to see you but was told you had been released into police custody.

So when I drove to London with Danielle and James's things on June 23, what a surprise. There you were with a big smile, bandages on your back, eating french fries and fooling around with the kids. When will you appear in court? Please let me know what is happening with you.

As you know when I left you I was crying. I was feeling discouraged and disheartened. There is a part of me that wants to grab you, shake you and scream, "Stop Killing Yourself!" Watching you is like watching a slow, macabre death with a laughing face. Then there is the ever haunting "What about the children?"

The summer days are beautiful here. I look at the swimming pool, and the grass, the flowers, and the toys I have saved and collected for my grandchildren. I feel sad that they do not feel connected enough to us to feel safe coming to visit.

I told you not long ago that I did not know how long we would be here. The company announced last week that the research centre will be closed by the end of 1993, which is six months from now. So Daddy is losing his job here and is waiting to hear if the company will move him somewhere else or lay him off. We are very disappointed by this news as we like it here and have just got the house looking beautiful.

Also, as I told you, if you decide you want help or support in kicking your addictions please ask for it before we are no longer here. Perhaps **want** is the wrong word. I imagine you **want** to keep having your cocaine and highs and pleasure and parties **and** your kids and success and family life, too. Can't have both, dear.

I do expect, one day, a phone call telling me you are dead. With all the other crazy phone calls, why not? I do feel an ache when I think of you, when you are in our life more and when you are in our life less.

When I do not hear from you, my imagination creates horrid stories and when I hear the craziness you have participated in I wonder what to do. So please do not cut me off and be clear about what you want from me. I will let you know, as before, whether doing what you ask is OK, or not, for me.

I am waiting to hear from you.

Love, Mom

August 4, 1993
Burlington, Ontario

My Dear Kelly

Thanks for calling me Sunday to let me know you are OK. I really appreciated your direct statement about being addicted to cocaine and alcohol. At least I do not have to put out any energy dealing with denial when you readily tell me your state of being and share some of your story. I do worry, what mother would not, with your apparent downhill interest in living. I worry so much about Danielle and James, too. Your biological mother abandoned you once. Danielle and James are left by you over and over—those addictions stealing you away. I could scream.

You told me that on Sunday you were going **holidaying** in Grand Bend. I did wonder, "Holidaying from what?" So I was surprised Monday when your Dad told me you had phoned from Victoria Hospital, something to do with kidneys and being tubed down with intravenous feeding, sharp pains in your stomach and back, and low blood pressure.

I phoned the hospital yesterday and today to see how you are. Today I was told you had left the hospital to go home. Is **home** still with someone called John?

I guess the guardian angel that I sent you is not doing a very effective job. A month ago it was a stab in your back and soon after that a leaky breast; now kidney problems. With all the alcohol I am surprised you are not having liver problems. I expect the kidney problem is diet and life style related. You are extremely rough on your beautiful body.

You deserve to treat yourself better; more tenderly, kindly, encouragingly and lovingly. NO! To what is not healthy and YES! To what is wise and HEALING. Your kids deserve better. For Danielle, you are the number one example of how to live a woman's life.

Kelly, live your life. I am willing and aching to help you.


Love to you, Mom

Jamie, Danielle and Kelly on the occasion of Les and Patricia's 25th Wedding Anniversary in 1993.

November 13, 1993
Burlington, Ontario

My dear Kelly

The last time I saw you was in August at our twenty fifth wedding anniversary. Your dad and I were so pleased that you came, with the children and your pleasant man friend. Danielle and James were great. I was glad you went to the trouble. I felt a loved mother and woman that day.

Since then your dad has been living mostly in Calgary and coming home when he can. Last month I went to Calgary and we bought our old house back; the one Uncle Jim designed. So that has been decided.

Katie and I are here alone a fair bit but we are getting along fine. She has her beginner's drivers license so we often go out driving.

Ben has started his Emergency Medical Training and loves his class, peers and teachers. He seems pleased that we are moving back.

When we talked on the phone in September I suggested that I would be comforted if you would go into addiction treatment. Your response was, "Didn't I tell you I go to AA?" Then I heard laughter in the background. Someone said, "Tell your mother you go to NA, too." And you did. Then I heard, "Tell her you belong to the PTA." You did and I heard more laughter. That is when I said, "I cannot carry on with this conversation," and hung up.

I wish and long for your membership in AA and NA. I would feel proud if you participated in the parent-teacher association and became involved in your children's education and future. I want you to know that I felt minimized and laughed at for wanting and longing for my daughter to get into recovery, to move into wellness and participation as a parent and community member. I do not know totally what is going on for you so I am left assuming that you are lost in **partying** and following the call of your addictions.

I am available if you want a hand to pull in a different direction, although Calgary will be a lot further away.

Kelly:
When you let your eyes see, they shine with wise knowing.
When you let your pain be felt, you show strength and softness.
When you hug and caress, you do it with deep appreciation.
And when you finally recognize how lovable and capable you are,
you will come back to my arms, recognizing, as never before,
that deep inside, where you feel small, scared, cuddly, hurt, sad, angry
and tender, you will always be our dear Kelly.

Love, Mom

February 22, 1994
Calgary, Alberta

Dearest Kelly

I was so sorry to hear that you are living through more pain and discomfort. I worry about the stress your body has endured. When I told Ben, he asked, "Are you sure she was not in another fight?" I said, "Kelly says she fell on ice." I imagine he was thinking of the time you broke your foot in a fight and told us you broke the top of your foot by stepping on a child's toy.

Anyway, no matter **how** you smashed the bones in your chin, I am sure the whole experience has been hard on you. Thanks for calling us to let us know what is happening. We hope you got the flowers we sent to the hospital.

Dad and I were pleased that you are thinking of going back to school. We have decided that if you send us receipts for courses, books or adult learning we will reimburse you.

Kelly, Dear Kelly, Oh! Dear Kelly,

All your dad and I want is for you to take good care of your:

• BODY by ingesting substances that nurture and listening and attending to your muscle, nerve and bone pains

• MIND by avoiding brain damaging drugs and filling your mind with encouraging messages: "I, Kelly, am deserving, lovable, capable of learning and growing."

• SOUL by loving your life and the energy that got you here.

• CHILDREN by doing all the above for Danielle and James until they can care for themselves.

May the Lord, indeed, be good and keep watch over you, since I cannot be close.

Love, Mom

March, 16, 1994
Calgary, Alberta

My dearest Kelly

You called last month to say your chin bones were broken. You were in a hospital and your mouth was going to be wired in position for six weeks. Dad and I sent flowers and I sent a letter. Where are you? How are you doing? Please call. Inbetween wondering if you are all right, wondering if you've moved into your own place, wondering if you've registered at Wheable School (the adult education school), I have continued house painting. Your Dad and I recently started wallpapering the kitchen/family room area. How I enjoy creating a beautiful home.

I have been seeing a career consultant to assess my skills and expertise. I may go back to school in September, stay active through volunteer work, or do a combination with part-time employment. I went to a volunteer interview for the Calgary Children's Festival in May. I am going to be a storyteller for two or three days. Oh, I wish you, James and Danielle could be here for that. Entertainers come here from all over the world.

I have been doing a bit of work with a parent and tots program in cooperation with the Native unit of Child Welfare. I have been to a sweet grass ceremony and enjoy the company of many of the Métis and Aboriginal people.

Last week I went to see a wildly funny play called **Sensible Footwear** by a group called Radical Feminists. They are from England. Three women were dressed in black tights with black tunics, singing jingles, telling jokes and doing mini skits about men leering at breasts, hips and lips, about bras, about vaginal infections, about having children, about Oprah and Vanna White and about cooking and cleaning. I laughed to almost wetting myself...but not, mind you.

Last night my friend, Linda and I went to the movie, **Mrs. Doubtfire**; wonderful. I cried and laughed. I've long admired Robin Williams. What a talented man.

You will be fascinated by this: Katie applied, was interviewed, provided two references and was accepted as a teen counsellor at the Calgary Drug/Distress Centre. She will be answering the phone and responding to crisis calls from teens. Monday she had a three hour information training on drugs. I thought of you. You could REALLY teach her about the issue. I gather the agency prefers to have recovering alcohol and drug users deal with using teens. Katie may meet some interesting young people. Once she is finished the training, she will be listening on the crisis line for six hours a week. Quite the commitment!

Your Dad's birthday was on Sunday. He is forty-seven years old. Eight of us, including Ben and Kate, went out for dinner. Ben said he could not join us until later and ten minutes after we arrived at the restaurant Star Bear came in with a bouquet of balloons, hugging your Dad and goofing around. Ben is volunteering as the Star Bear mascot for Stars, a rescue helicopter program. Star Bear is a great big guy with a leather jacket and goggles.

I have discovered a marvelous book called **The Joy of Not Working** by Ernie Zelinsky. You might look for it the next time you are in your local library. It is for people who do not know how best to use their leisure time, are workaholics and for those partly or totally unemployed. Ernie talks about establishing a routine, purpose and community to have a fulfilling life. He uses humour, interesting facts and quotes, some Zen ideas and some fun exercises.

Hope this reaches you somewhere warm.

All my love, Mom

April 18, 1994
Calgary, Alberta

My dear Kelly

You phoned last week and told Katie you were in jail. I am glad you called. Maybe you will have an opportunity to attend AA, eat and get healthy. Anyway, I am glad you called. It was more than two months ago that you called to tell us about the operation on your jaw and I am still wondering how that went for you.

Katie said you would call this Sunday. Obviously, we did not hear from you. So I am feeling disappointed about that.

I find it hard. I feel frustrated that we do not have an address or telephone number where you can be reached. That leaves you totally in charge of making contact with us, other than I write these letters addressed to Lillian and trust that they eventually get to you. Sometimes, I wonder about that because it seems as if I write and write with little response.

I miss the children. I could call Lillian's more often to talk on the phone with them. That seems to have limited success especially if they are not in the mood to chat with me and that is, if they even remember me.

Do you remember Liz and Balder VanStam? She used to direct the Early Childhood Education program at Lambton College. They spent last weekend with us on their three month trip across Canada. They are older and retired now. Your Dad and I had fun with them talking and wandering along the Elbow River in Bragg Creek looking for unusual and suggestively shaped stones.

Wherever you are, whatever you are doing or not doing, whoever you are with, know that we think of you.

Do let me know, Kelly, if I can support you around taking on your demons; your addictions, fears and haunting past.

Love to you, Mom

April 23, 1994
Calgary, Alberta


My dear Kelly

I imagine you may be feeling let down by us and angry that we said "no" to your request for lending you five hundred dollars for bail. I want you to know that your Dad and I spent a long time talking and soul searching before we decided. We took your situation seriously. We did feel surprised and confused when Thursday after we said "no" you said that the charges were being dropped and you would be released from jail Monday, anyway. We asked "What is the panic for bail money about?" I guess you will be out of jail by the time you receive this letter.

We heard from you in February about your shattered jaw, then no word from you for two months and then three phone calls in three days, after a short conversation with Katie the Saturday before.

We have decided, Kelly, that we want to avoid in any way acting as enablers. We do not want to support your present lifestyle. I told you last summer that we were going to be much more cautious about the kind of **help** we give you. We fear ending up resenting that our **investments** disappear and make no difference. From our viewpoint your decisions look less and less responsible and healthy in the last year or so.

As your Dad said to you: "It does not matter if, since you declared your independence from us, that we have lent or given you twenty, two hundred, two thousand or twenty thousand dollars." We experience the money we have given you in the past making no healthy, progressive difference in your life. Sometimes we have even asked ourselves: "Have we contributed to the bashing of her body and life with the money we have given her? How much money has been spent on drugs, alcohol and cigarettes? If we had not provided money, clothes, a cheque here and there for rent and utilities maybe our Kelly would not have ingested as much brain and life killing substances into her body."

You told me once that you **chickened**, or whatever the phrase is, six times requiring the ambulance to come to revive you after overdosing on cocaine. You have also told me that you do not need to go into addiction treatment. Kelly, I believe you will never make it out of the lifestyle of partying and jail visiting until you take treatment and counselling seriously. Actually, a part of your Dad's and my conversation consisted of reflecting on the fact that we feel less worry when you are in jail. We do not worry as much about your safety. We do not worry about you overdosing on drugs, spinning about in stolen cars, being stabbed or raped. We said we realized how angry you were in jail but at least you had fewer ways to come closer to killing yourself. Of course, we know, you do not want to be in jail, but we ask: "She wants to get out to do what?"

The difference with you out of jail is that I feel afraid more. In jail we know you can eat, can attend AA meetings and we won't be waiting for the phone call saying, "I am sorry to tell you, Mr. and Mrs. Morgan that your daughter Kelly died of..." Loving you is hard on us, whether we say "yes" or "no." Then we struggle with the guilt that goes along with the chosen "yes" or "no."

Last fall I felt hurt when you made fun of the idea of getting addiction help. Your Dad and I did not laugh when you called crying and wanting to get bail money. We heard your pain. We talked about your pain and ours. Jail bail is not the kind of help we want to or will give. What you laughed at is the kind of support we are willing to give.

We want to keep loving you, Kelly, and we have decided we need the freedom to say "no" to you. And it is not easy. We heard the anger in your voice. That is understandable.

I feel so sad about all the losses:
• all the fine brains, reading and writing power, high energy, creativity, humour and loving appreciation in you
• James and Danielle worn and torn emotionally in so many ways
• you, taken away by your addictive habits from those who love you.

I think of all the people who could more easily connect to you if you were living productively and healthily; giving to the world of your caring and bright qualities. Such a waste. Such a loss. I grieve. I have done a lot of grieving, of many losses, in this last year. Yet I also feel hope.

All that good stuff of Kelly Morgan is still there deep inside. No one stole that. The story is not over. One day when you are ready, I believe, you will light your light and the world around you will celebrate.

With love, Mom

June 8, 1994
Calgary, Alberta

Dear Kelly

We have not heard from you in nearly two months. I miss you. Are you feeling angry when you think of us? It is probably time I stopped trying to figure you out. I was not very successful when you were close and I saw you more often.

I hope you are OK. Actually, I hope you are better than OK. I hope you are putting the pieces of your life together.

I miss Danielle and James. How are they?

I will be in England with your Dad next week and will then be in Ontario for a bit. I need to see your Grandma Mary. She and I miss one another very much. I do not see how I can get to London to see the children. I am sorry about that. Please give them my love if you see them.

Please consider giving us a call collect, as ever.

I do hope this gets to you. Gee! I am doing a lot of hoping when it comes to you. I do have much "hope" for you. The story is not over, yet.

You are twenty-six years old. I wonder. Is your life a quarter over and you will live to one hundred and four years? Is it one third over and you'll live to seventy-eight years or, heaven forbid, half over? Then you would live to fifty-two years. No matter, you are still a young woman. At your age I was a young mother with Ben hardly a year old and I had not met you yet.

Here I go again. I hope, you create a birthday that pleases you, to mark the day you entered the world. I bet you arrived head first.

I am planning to send off a little parcel to you and **hope** it gets to you by your birthday. I also **hope** you still pick up your correspondence through Lillian.

When I cannot do much because of distance and not knowing how to reach you, I make do with what is available to me, writing to you and **hoping**.


Love to you, dear, Mom

September 6, 1994
Calgary, Alberta


My dear Kelly

I called you this morning at the jail, The Vanier Institute for Women. The receptionist said he would give you the message that you could call collect. It is ten p.m. I waited home all day. You did not call. I feel disappointed.

I have called Lillian and the children a couple of times this summer to see how they and you are. In one conversation they said you had not picked up my letters and they have not seen you for a while.

Then last week I called again. Danielle told me "Mommy is in jail." So I called the London jail and was told you were being transferred to Brampton. They kindly gave me the phone number and address. I felt quite hopeful when I heard that this facility has a treatment program. I sure hope you get the help and support you deserve.

Please let me know if you would like some photos, old ones of yourself, some of the children or ones of us.

Katie is in Grade twelve and is talking about aiming for a science program in university. She works each Tuesday night at Pizza Hut twisting balloon animals for the children in the restaurant. She continues to entertain as Sassy, the clown, at children's birthday parties. Yes! She still suffers from **princess syndrome**, holds her nose a bit too high and reads for long hours in her extremely messy bedroom with the door firmly closed.

Ben is in love with a twenty-five year old elementary school teacher. They play and snuggle around in a sweet way. He is waiting to be placed for his hours on an ambulance so that he can finish his Emergency Medical Technician training. He is burning out after three years of being a law firm **photocopy boy**.

Your Dad is unhappy in his daily work. The company seems to have a more aggressive attitude than in the past. So we try to make evenings and weekends pleasant. Actually he and three men friends, are going away to Bowron Lakes in British Columbia this month for a week of canoeing. That will be a sweet perk for him.

Me? I miss you. And Ontario, and Danielle and James. And my mom. She is not all that well. I volunteer here and there. I have joined Toastmasters to keep practiced in speaking. I am taking facilitator training in an interesting eight week course called Developing Capable People.

Have got to go. Please call.

Love, Mom


September 7, 1994
Calgary, Alberta

Dear Kelly,

Well! I called Vanier again this morning. This time I learned that Timberlea is an assessment unit and then you will be assigned to a program. They have many programs. I also learned that when I leave my phone number you cannot call until four p.m. or after. That is two p.m. or after our time in Calgary.

Kelly, I have no idea how you arrived in jail again and, as far as sending my love, it makes no difference. I just hope you can put some life pieces together for yourself. I imagine you have been hurting far too long.

My love, Mom

September 8, 1994
Calgary, Alberta

Thanks Kelly

For returning my call of this morning. So you were wondering if something dreadful had happened to one of us, otherwise, you were not going to call. I am interested in what has kept you away from saying "hello" for so long. I am sorry our time on the phone was so quick. Fifteen minutes is not long enough when we have not really talked since February. Our three short phone conversations in April were stressed by the focus on the bail issue.

Thanks for saying "I love you" when we had to hang up tonight. I felt a piece of you come back to me.

Thanks for answering your Dad's questions so openly and telling me about how well you did in that London Addiction program. Then you told me about losing your thirty-two days of sobriety after you went **partying** on your birthday. The truth has a truthful ring to it.

I feel so proud that you went thirty-two days. I am only sorry that I could not have known about that time and encouraged you. You can do it again, if you want, but then you know that.

Please consider writing me and filling me in on your life, thoughts, desires, dreams, whatever. I have invested a fair bit into your life. I would like a catch up on progress made so far. Never forget that you are important and special to me.

Love, Mom

September 9, 1994
Calgary, Alberta

Dear Kelly,

I heard from Ben that I missed your call last night. He said he had a good talk with you and he has written you a letter.

So, he asked if you would like a couple of months out here to get really **cleaned out** and start fresh. You are most welcome if you would like to be in some addiction program. Ben would be most supportive. Me too!

We had imagined that you were picked up by the police for some drug problem. It is so much easier when you let us know what is really going on with you. So thank you again for telling us what is happening in your life.

We do not blame you. You are not the first person on earth, in North America, in Canada, in our family to be hooked on a substance addiction. We can hear how hard it is for you. Sometimes it takes many, many attempts: start, stop, start, stop, until people get clear about what they can consume, who is supportive, who is trouble, what they really want in life, how to get it, what is stopping them, and why they fear feeling pain. Complicated.

Please let us know if we have any way to help you be stronger in facing your addictions. Ben says you asked for some photos and pretty pictures. Please find some enclosed.

Love, Mom

September 26, 1994
Calgary, Alberta

Dear Kelly

I phoned Vanier Institute today and I learned that you have been transferred back to London. I called the London detention centre and they will not pass my phone messages to you. All I can do is write you and ask you to phone me.

Kelly, will you please call me—us?

I sent you paper and a stamped envelope when you were at Vanier's. I also sent another letter, photos, pictures and Benjamin's letter. Did you receive these? Ben is wondering, too, if you received his letter.

I was told that you probably went back to London to face some additional charges. So, I have been thinking about you and wondering. Please do not forget that we care about you. What you did, you did. How is our Kelly now?

We are all healthy and quite busy. I am getting busier and, with walking most days, I am feeling fairly fit. Give us a call, sweetie.

Love, Mom

**To the reader:** In the following letter I heard for the first time some of Kelly's deep pain. Her disclosing words still bring tears of tenderness from my heart.

September 21, 1994 (received September 28)
London Detention Centre, London, Ontario

Dear Mom

Thank you so much for your letters. They are my favourite letters I ever received from you. Maybe, for a change, my head is clear enough to comprehend the real love with which they are written, (and concern). Mom, I won't get help this time at Vanier's as I won't be there long enough for their treatment. Also I got sent back to London.

Here is what is going on.

Back in July, I was the passenger in a truck which got pulled over. The cop told me he wanted to search my purse (which is illegal search and seizure as I wasn't under arrest for anything at the time). Anyway I had a crack pipe in my purse (which is used to smoke crack cocaine). Anyway the cop took it and said he would send it away for analysis. He told me if any of the drug was found in the pipe he would charge me for possession of a narcotic. Well I pretty much forgot all about it as time went by.

But the analysis just came back, or they waited to charge me. They have up to three months. So I was just charged today, September 21, for this. It is a dirty trick on their part as they waited till I'm almost done my time to charge me so I would have to start my new time all over again. But the charge will be withdrawn, when I go to my two hour trial on October 12.

So, Mom if you wonder why I just explained it all when you wouldn't know the difference as I won't get extra time, it's because, Mom, I never give you a chance, by letting you know what's up, and respecting you enough to let you decide what to do with the information. Does this make any sense? I'm not sure if I put my feelings into words right as I am not used to this all, so I may have a bit of trouble in this letter. But I'm going to try.

Mom, these are the things that brought tears to my eyes and why: #1 Just you writing to me and that you called EMDC jail, Vanier's receptionist two times. From this I see how much trouble and time you went to locate your daughter. Me. You wrote about James telling you I'm in jail. I imagined you could feel pain for James as well as James' pain.

I am too. I feel unbelievable guilt, Mom. But I always push it away as I am not good at feeling pain without masking it with drugs and booze, and haven't for many, many years. I was smoking joints with Chris and her brother since Grade eight at Hanna Public school. But I will get into that at another time if you want to with me.

Anyway, to get back on track. You wrote that you hope I get the help and support "THAT I DESERVE." Mom not once in my entire life have I let myself look at it that way. Mom, I am extremely irresponsible. But down inside I don't feel I deserve to help myself. I haven't, since before you adopted me. YOU tried so hard to make me feel special which is why Ben and Katie do. You did the right things, Mom, but it was too late. Too much damage was done to me before I got to you. I know this for a fact. I don't know anything particular, events or anything. It may have been nothing terrible happened at all, but something hurt me real bad when I was young, very young and that is how it has been ever since. A lot of pain and confusion my whole life. That scares me very much because look what I am doing to my own children. God help me, why? This is something I don't know. It sounds like such a cop out, but Mom, can you believe it's out of control? You may roll your eyes at that. You may not but I can't explain it any other way. Why would someone that loved their kids as much as I do be doing what I'm doing? Can you explain it? Anyway back on track again.

As you can probably tell, I am reading your letter again, as I go along.

You say Dad is unhappy at work. That is pretty major. How is it affecting your life, Mom? That must be hard on you, too. Your Mom, my grandma, isn't well. I know how much you love your Mom. You must be worried.

They would not give me any magazine clippings you sent. But they are in my property for when I get out.

You waited home all day for me to call. Mom, I'm truly sorry now that I didn't. That was IMMATURE and SELFISH that I didn't consider your feelings.

One of the main things that made me start crying is you wrote "I have no idea how you ended up there and it doesn't matter." I feel unconditionally loved when I read this. I feel I don't have to explain my actions, which is usually how I MAKE MYSELF FEEL. I don't know why. But you remember how often I would lie when there was no point to it. As if I thought something terrible would happen if I didn't. I did this before I ever got to you and Dad, I believe. Why?

You also wrote "I imagine you've been hurting far too long." How did you know this? I am just realizing it myself. NO, not realizing it, admitting it to me.

I am also kind of scared of the love I feel for James and Danielle. As if I can't get too close to any human, even my own children. It is, as if, a part of me feels that if I love anyone, they will be taken away from me, or I will be taken away from them. I don't really understand it myself. I'm scared that I will never find answers to my questions. Too much happens, too young. I have no idea why, but I feel I was destroyed by the time I was five. I don't know why, Mom, as for all I know they could've been good foster homes I was in. But I sure as hell know that somewhere, somehow, sometime, SOMETHING went wrong. I may never know what. So, I guess I just have to get over it, or I am a write off? But I have no right to abandon my children. I am doing to them what was done to me. Why?

You thanked me for saying "I love you." I didn't even think you heard me.

WELL. I do love you very deeply. You are my one and only MOM. I am your daughter. We have lived our life together as nobody else has exactly. You don't have the exact same relationship with anybody else as me, right? Does that make any sense?

Another main thing is you told me you were PROUD, that I went thirty-two days. I didn't want to tell you in the first place because, Mom, I didn't want to fail and let you down again. Even if I had been sober a year and failed, I would have rather you never knew than show you yet another failure of mine.

But you said that you were "proud of my thirty-two day's PERIOD." I thought it would seem so petty to you. So what, thirty-two days, when she has screwed up with the rest of her life. But this is not fair of me to judge you like that, so I shared my small success with you and you were PROUD OF ME! You don't know how that made me feel. It's not at all that I want a pat on the back. That's not it. I just didn't want to feel like a dismal failure once again, which is how I make myself feel. I am very hard on myself emotionally. You and Dad may find that hard to believe, but it is true.

You said you felt a piece of me come back to you. Well, Mom, I need you, I love you and I'm scared because I know you won't be there for me forever. So, I push myself away, thinking that way I will not be devastated if anything ever happened to you. Another thing I learned when I was young? I seem to do it with anybody who comes close to my heart.

You say I'm important and special to you. You have always told me that. I am just, for once, letting myself feel like that. Maybe it's just a fluke day and I don't know why after all these years I'm writing my true feelings to you. Mom, you deserve so much better from me. I can't ever say anything will change. No more promises to me or anyone else. Making promises to myself and you when I screw up and feel like a fuck up. It sets me back so much further. Why?

I just know that's the way it is. Not fair to me or you, huh? Well, Mom, I am emotionally drained for the night, so I will shut my feelings off for awhile as I have always done. I feel like I have been through the wringer and I'm not used to it. But I want you to know that you are loved by me very much. I also love Dad so much, Mom. I am very, very proud of him, for the person that he is. I wish so much that I had some of his qualities. Why can't I make myself responsible, caring, mature, loving like him? I often wonder this. And Dad deserves to be told this. Someday I hope I can tell him, but I don't feel he'd believe me. Wouldn't blame him. Actually, just show him this part of the letter. Sometimes I think Dad just thinks I am just plain lazy and irresponsible. This is true, but seriously something is definitely wrong with me, also. I know it's my responsibility to find out what. I know that. I assume Dad thinks "Well, why the hell doesn't she do something about it?" This is a very good question!

Well Mom, I'm going to wrap this up, as this is about as much as I can handle in one sitting. I'm not used to feeling much of anything. I can't phone you as they won't give me my phone book out of my property since I was transferred back and you can't dial information from any jail. PLEASE SEND YOUR PHONE #. I want pictures very badly of you all, and my children. Maybe even one of me. But I only want a duplicate as I am sick of my losing things, things that mean a lot to me. SO, I know it's asking a lot but I would appreciate it. We are allowed six pictures per cell. Also cards brighten up my cell immensely. You always pick such special cards. If you feel like it, I would love one or two.

Well, Mom, I love you dearly and I hope very much that I allow myself to write to you like this again. I feel as if the Mom I love (YOU) is in the same room as me right now.

Goodnight!

Love, Kelly (whew!)

P.S: So far my release date is October 21. I'll keep you posted.

Love, Kelly

October 3, 1994
Calgary, Alberta

My dear Kelly

I received your letter on Friday. Kelly, I read it and felt amazed, touched, loved, enlightened and I cried from a tender spot. I was enlightened to the fact that you are aware of much more than I imagined.

Your letter was like having heavy drapes drawn from a window. I have been in the dark room about you. You have sent light by sharing with me your truth, Kelly's truth. Your letter was full of feelings that were truths from your heart.

You may close up again. You may close down a lot or a little or stay open, but I will always have your sixteen pages to warm me. I feel glad that you are realizing that I am able, most moments—after all I am human—to love all of you. You do not have to hide anymore, at least you did not in your letter. I want to respond to so much of what you said.

You said "I'm not sure if I put my feelings into words right as I am not used to this." Sweetie, when it comes to your feelings, there is no right or wrong. They just are. They tell you who you are, what's important to you, what you want and don't want, what's pleasurable and painful to you. Basically feelings are energy moving through your body. Drugs and alcohol deaden that moving, deaden the feelings. Then you said, "But I'm going to try" and what a beautiful and inspiring result.

You wrote, "I feel unbelievable guilt, Mom." I feel so proud of you. You feel guilty with regard to Danielle and James. I feel glad that you feel guilt, that you regret some of your decisions and actions that most definitely have affected them. That guilty feeling can motivate you to decide differently in the future. It is OK Kelly. You are OK Kelly. It is healthy to feel guilt when you make a big mistake. It tells me that you want things different.

I want to tell you that when you wrote "I am not good at feeling pain," I thought "Hey, it is tough for most of us, including me." I used to sleep a lot or have yelling rages, sometimes hitting you, when I was not willing to feel my **own** pain. So, you have used booze and drugs to mask your pain. Most of us have some form that we developed to cope with overwhelming pain. You coped the best you could.

You've been smoking joints since grade eight! Wow! Was I naive? I believed I could stop you, if I really tried, from smoking cigarettes when you were in grade nine and ten. That is a long involvement with drugs. But, as you know from your AA meetings, the years toward sobriety build a day at a time. Today is the beginning of the rest of your life, my dear.

Of course "you deserve" treatment. You deserve a life, hope, laughter and tears, health and your Mama's potato salad. And you particularly, deserve your children in your arms.

You wrote "down inside I don't feel I deserve to help myself. I haven't since before you adopted me." I had imagined that was your belief. We had a conversation once where you basically confirmed my fear that you were slowly killing yourself. That "down inside," I believe, is a wounded Kelly from when you were a little girl. You were so very badly hurt that you stayed tight inside, feeling afraid to get close. Your letter is an enormous opening. Please believe this.

You wrote "You did the right things, Mom." I made many mistakes, hid my own feelings, lashed out, felt guilty and I did and do love you.

You wrote "but it was too late. Too much damage was done to me before I got to you." Kelly, I believe and I want you to believe that "it is never too late." My dad died, I felt OK about him and I had forgiven him. I used to hate him so much for the **damage** he did to me, some, of which, I passed on to you.

And Kelly, I've worked with many very hurt and "damaged" people, some of whom had been drugged up and alcoholic into their thirties and forties. They have asked for help and changed. Many of them had no one there for them. Some even had families that continued to violate them. I am not blaming you, dear. I am trying to offer hope. No one is **too damaged**. You certainly were not unlovable to us. You were lovable since we met you. All children are lovable.

You wrote "something hurt me real bad when I was young, very young." That's what all that therapy for you, as a child, was about. We were all waiting for you to come out and tell us about your fears and pain. But you were a very scared little girl. It certainly didn't help when you had to live in a residential home for over a year when Katie was born. The school and I were having trouble keeping up with you. That must have been hard on you. I know it was on me.

You mentioned once about a teenage boy getting into bed with you when you lived at the foster home. I asked if you suspected sexual abuse. You mentioned a lighter lit under your hand when reaching into a cookie jar. I know the foster parents used to hit you with a wooden spoon for wetting your bed. Pretty nasty stuff.

I've done inner child work many years for myself, mostly around Grandpa Ted. I've helped others with it. You are beginning inner healing. I see it in your letter. I see the awareness. I see willingness to feel, to ask questions and wonder. The more you remember, I believe, the more you will continue to remember. It is healing to feel the feelings and acknowledge that they rest in the past. It is OK to feel pain and cry, feel scared and tremble, feel angry at the outrages and inflictions and yell, hit a pillow or write an angry letter. Of course this is much easier to do with a safe person supporting you; like a wise friend, safe counsellor or therapist.

The more you remember and feel, the more you will continue to remember and feel. And the better you will get at being, that is **being** with your feelings.

That's healing.

You wrote, "God help me." God will. God is. I believe God is the loving goodness that breathed life into you. Turn inside to that breath, the one place in your body where there's peace and God will help.

You wrote, "it's out of control." I expect you feel out of control when you are afraid to feel and shut down the feelings. That has been my experience.

You wrote, "Why would someone that loved their kids as much as I do be doing what I'm doing? Can you explain it?" You answered this yourself Kelly when you wrote, "I'm also kind of scared of the love I feel for James and Danielle. As if I can't get too close to any human…it's as if a part of me feels that if I love anyone, they will be taken away from me." Abandonment was a prime theme in your formative years when basic beliefs about yourself and the world were forming. As a baby you were probably close to your biological mother and, at about eighteen months, you were permanently taken away from her. You lived with foster parents. You probably made some attachments there. You were taken away. You were three years old when you were supposedly adopted by a family that said they would love you forever. After about eight months they sent you back to the foster home. I feel incredible rage towards these people. What a thing to do! "I'll be your Mommy. I'll be your Daddy." Then "No. We've changed our minds. We are sending you away." We were never given any information about that adoptive family. Apparently you really regressed, wet your bed and sucked on a baby bottle when you were sent back to the foster home. Then when you were five years old you met us and moved in at five and half years. You've been told this information before but, perhaps, it has a new meaning for you, with your new wonderings and realizations.

So, of course, the little unconscious part of you believes that if you get close "they will be taken away." I want to comfort that abandoned, little part of you. Kelly, you were promised safety and love many times and it was taken away from you. Oh Kelly, how I have longed to support you in sorting out those injuring messages you collected.

It makes perfect sense that for you, as a little girl, you made a decision to not let people get too close. It kept you safe. You needed to survive. You were and are so smart. That decision is not working for you anymore, that's all. It doesn't work to push away your children. What a perplexing place to be. Probably the lying is part of the same theme. I imagine, as a little kid, you believed that if you were seen as imperfect we'd remove the love and send you away.

I feel so glad that you are "admitting" that you feel hurt. How did I know you've been hurting for a long time? We knew there was all kinds of things we didn't know or understand when you came to us. Then, I have learned that under every addiction is pain and hurt being drowned. I know it for myself and others. You wrote, "Admitting it to me." Good going dear. It's your life and the number one person with whom to be truthful is yourself. I admire the soul searching you have done.

Yes, I love you. My love does not change because you are in jail. I care about your life. I want you to know that I prefer a healthy and growing Kelly and your letter reflected a lot of truth and health. It does matter to me if you are breaking the law and how you are caring for, or not, Danielle and James. The point is **no matter what** I love you. Thank you for getting that message. I was impressed that you recognized "unconditional love."

You wrote, "I'm scared that I will never find answers to my questions." Feel scared and ask. You have begun, anyway. You have taken steps. Add your thirty two days of sobriety in the spring to your beginnings.

You wrote, "I feel I was destroyed by the time I was five." I believe you had relationships, a biological upbringing, hopes, and days destroyed. They were not grieved. You were not allowed to weep and grieve all those very young losses. You received the message "Smile, act sweet, as if all is well, so the next adopting family will keep you." I'm guessing, of course. You decide what rings true for you.

You wrote: "I sure as hell know that somewhere, somehow, sometime, something went wrong." Absolutely!

You wrote "I guess I just have to get over it, or I am a write off." Maybe it is more "get through it," dear, and you do that by doing just what you are doing. You have so clearly identified and named your wounds.

You wrote, "I abandoned my children. I am doing to them what was done to me." I believe it relates to your belief from being very little, "get close and you will be taken away from me."

No, I do not have the exact same relationship with anybody else. You are my **chosen** daughter and you are very special to me. If I had not had you in my life I would not be as wise and loving as I am. I would probably still be some church basement version of Miss Romper Room who hadn't been challenged to look at her patterns and evolve. You have been my biggest teacher. You taught me "I can change no one but myself." I tried to force you to share your feelings and to tell the truth. I would get frustrated and eventually when you were about fifteen I finally got it. I had to love myself, change myself, let you go and wait until you asked for help.

Do you see how important your letter was to me?

Yes, I feel proud of you when you take any steps forward. When a toddler falls it does not take away from the steps made.

You wrote "I am very hard on myself emotionally." Most people are harder on themselves internally, than the external world, me included. When you were little and you had big giant people come down on you, as I suspect happened, those adult voices become internalized. They go deep inside you but you forget. It is called unconscious. I hear that you are starting to acknowledge that you have these put down voices in your head. Well you could start to recognize them as old and not so caring or smart adult voices. Then say "Shut up" to them. It is time for you to challenge these old demons.

You are doing the best you can.

I will love you no matter what.

Making mistakes is OK

Tomorrow we will start again.

Aw, you wrote, "I need you, I love you, I'm scared because I know you won't be there for me forever." I feel the same way about my Mom. I intend to be around for about another forty years. The odds look very good to me. Yes, your pushing away so separation will not be so devastating is a real theme. You need all the goodies you can get from me in the next four decades. Would you like an hour of pure cuddling with me saying "Kelly, I believe you are lovable and capable?"

I feel so glad that you wrote that you are "letting myself feel that (special)." There is only one of you, Kelly. I have only met one you, irreplaceable you.

Don't fuss about "**why** after all these years I am writing my true feelings." Questions such as How? When? For whom? are easier. Maybe twenty-six years was enough to wait. I do not know but thank God. Thank God you wrote your letter of TRUE FEELINGS.

I have waited twenty years to see and hear you.

You wrote, "I can't ever say anything will change." HEY! Yoo Hoo! Kelly! This is big change. Your letter is enormous, feeling, honest, sharing, connecting, soul searching, wondering and loving.

You wrote "I am emotionally drained for the night, so I will shut my feelings off for a while as I have always done. I feel like I have been through the wringer and I'm not used to it." Shutting down emotionally probably helped you survive those very painful early years. You are a survivor, as they say. Your ability to shut down is a strength, if used appropriately. It is one strength you share with your Dad. Although he has learned to share his feelings more in the last ten or so years.

I so appreciate and feel honoured that you shared this "going through the wringer" with me, that you experienced me as a safe person to be open with and "as if I was in the room."

I feel your love Kelly. Thank you.

So does your Dad. He finds it harder to respond. Thanks for understanding that. I showed him your letter and he may write you.

I have enclosed some things for you.

Did you not get that package with pictures, cards and photos that I sent to Vaniers? I feel disappointed if not. So, I will try again. I also sent you writing paper for you to write Danielle and James.

I was thinking of the Twelve Steps in AA. Your letter covers many of the steps, Kelly. I felt amazed and impressed. You have taken a big step.

- **Step One**

  We admitted we were powerless over alcohol—that our lives had become unmanageable.
  — You used the phrase "out of control."

- **Step Two**

  Came to believe that a Power greater than ourselves could restore us to sanity.
  — You wrote "God help me."

- **Step Three**

  Made a decision to turn our will and our lives over to the care of God as we understand him.
  — You wrote "God help me."

- **Step Four**

  Made a searching and fearless moral inventory of ourselves.
  — You wrote about your weaknesses, abandonment of your children and letting us and yourself down.

- **Step Five**

  Admitted to God, to ourselves, and to another human being the exact nature of our wrongs.
  — You sure admitted a pile of mistakes in your letter.

• **Step Eight**

Made a list of all persons we had harmed and became willing to make
amends to all of them.

— You sure made amends with me, dear, and Dad, too.


Ben says that I may share with you that at age nineteen years he remembered that when he was seven or eight years old he went off to a church camp for a week with a friend. He was sexually abused by a camp counsellor who coerced him into promising never to tell. He remembered four years ago. It was hard on us all but he is healed up and would be willing to talk to you about it if that would be helpful.

I truly hope you will allow yourself to write or talk about this openly again. Your letter is the largest and most meaningful gift you have ever given me, a significant and truthful sharing of yourself.

We are willing to discuss the possibility of you coming out here to attend a treatment program if you feel ready and believe that would be helpful. A number of years ago you had a brief stay in a treatment centre and you asked me then if I knew anything about inner child work. The counsellor there was encouraging you but the situation didn't work for you. You now sound ready. Nevertheless, you will need to decide when, how, where and with whom.


My love is with you, Mom.

October 8, 1994
Calgary, Alberta

Dear Kelly

We talked twice yesterday on the phone. You sounded so clear and available. I experienced my heart just opening wide to you and your Dad's warming and expanding. He really heard your "I love you, Dad." Your friend, Dee sounds like a wonderful and healthy support to you. You are smart. You know who will encourage you to go in what direction.

Please think about whether you would like to come to Calgary for a couple of weeks before Christmas. You could take back some parcels for the children. You have lots of options. I feel glad that you realize that it is your responsibility to look into counselling. Dr. Hasswell sounds like a wise connection for you when you get out. I am comforted to know that she is a caring professional you trust.

I also felt pleased to hear about your latest grade eleven credit. Your education record could be very helpful to you in the future. Have the teacher forward it to me if you want me to keep it safe.

I asked you to call Monday. I forgot that we will be at John Scholten's birthday party. Maybe you will get Katie and you two can share a few stories.

You told me about beginning to remember your childhood, wondering, asking about what happened to you and wanting to put the clues together to explain your present beliefs and behaviours. I am convinced, truly convinced, that you have begun to heal yourself. I encourage you to continue to write me. I have enclosed some information written by a woman called Jean Illsley Clarke (Refer to Appendix I). Look at what little children need to receive at different ages to grow and feel loved. You may cry and feel angry when you read the list and realize all that you did not get. That is OK. You felt outraged when I told you about Ben's abuse. It is time to feel infuriated at what was done to you. The more anger you place where it belongs, in it's proper angry home, the more you will find your anger is expressed appropriately. I imagine, when you struggle with containing your anger, the person on the other end of your fist is receiving much of your old and repressed anger.

Yes, Daddy and I have both gone to therapy and are learning more to accept ourselves. I have learned that the more I accept and love myself the easier it is to accept and love others. I have luckily had my mother supportively listen to me most of my life. I feel honoured to do so for you. I only hope that you will continue to leave the door open for me and your family's love.

Love, Mom

October 10, 1994
Calgary, Alberta

Thanksgiving: I give thanks for you, Kelly.

**You cannot be at peace with yourself until you realize happiness
with life is part smiles and part tears. (Anonymous)**

Dear Kelly

Lillian called to ask if I had located and connected with you. She asked me to ask you to send a letter, a note, some word to James and Danielle. They miss you dreadfully.

James actually spoke to me on the phone and told me he would like gymnastic lessons. I have asked Lillian to look into the possibility and it would give your Dad and me pleasure to pay the fee. I bet he would be wonderful at it, just like his double jointed, flexible and muscle bound mother was as a young gymnast.

Rhyming, writing, gymnastics, music; you have so many strengths.

Please stay out of that solitary hole place, dear.


My love, Mom

October 27, 1994
Calgary, Alberta

Dear Kelly

Last week when I came home from a night class, your Dad told me that you had called, something to the effect that we would not hear from you for a while because you were going into the hole or digger. How dreadful! When I asked him, "why did she get sent there, again?" he said he did not know. I thought you were getting out of jail last Friday, so I have been waiting and expecting a phone call.

This morning I wanted to know where you were. I called Elgin Middlesex Detention Centre. I was told "yes" you were there and "no" they could not pass on a message to you. So, I said, "Then I will write."

I sure hope you are OK.

I think of you every day,

As my mother thinks of me,

As I imagine, you do, of your children.

Ben is away now for three weeks in Bonnyville, Alberta, six hours drive away, doing his EMT. I enjoy seeing him stay so persistent with his goal.

Nothing much has changed for your Dad at work. He is hanging in there, hoping to reach retirement eligibility in three to five years. We are both happy with our involvement in a new thought church, The Centre for Positive Living. Your Dad goes to a class Thursday nights studying the writings of Ralph Waldo Emerson. On Tuesday's, I attend a class on basic spiritual ideas and meditation. Sunday we go to service together. Sometimes Ben comes. Katie sleeps in.

I am loving the children I work with in a native community here in the city. I work Monday and Tuesday in the playroom. I am doing a bit of counselling and attend professional speaking classes.

Please, Kelly, take care of yourself in all the ways you are able. Remember, you are loved. We offer support and will help you. I have been touched and feeling connected to you through your letter and recent open and caring phone calls. Keep me in your heart, dear.

Love, Mom

November 9, 1994
Calgary, Alberta

My dear Kelly,

You called last week, after ten days in that jail "hole" for being involved in a fight. You were out of jail and drinking with "a friend." He did not sound like much of a friend to me. I felt worried about you, especially after your overdose of speed and drinking with your "friend," bringing up blood and bile and being sought by the police for additional charges. I want to hear the truth. Please do not believe that I want us to go back to "Kelly pretending life is cool" in the crack houses and slums. I care and want better for you. I do worry.

You said you would call your lawyer, whom you trust, to figure out what you should do next.

I feel disappointed that your friend, Dee, and you did not go to her cottage. I, as your mother, liked that plan. I also was hoping to hear back from you this weekend.

I'll send this note off in care of Lillian, as usual. You said you took the children out on Halloween and the three of you cried about being together. I trust you will continue to connect with them. They need you in their life and "yes" absolutely I see change. I like your new, open and honest talk.

My love, Mom

December 30, 1994
Calgary, Alberta

Dear Kelly,

I felt so glad to hear your voice on Christmas Day. Thank you for calling. We think of you. We wonder how you are, especially when we don't hear from you for long stretches. Contact with you is important to us. Two months, actually since late October, was a long time for me. I end up worrying about you and our relationship when I do not hear from you.

I notice how I feel when you do not call and then I wonder in what ways Danielle and James are affected by your long absences, your disappearances. Please, Kelly, for your sake, their sake, our sake please consider fighting your addiction and getting well. Realistically, I understand that you need to serve your jail term before you can consider a treatment program.

I believe you deserve a plan for your life. Have you thought of your life plan? What about a plan for your children's future? Does it include you? In what ways? Does your children's future include us and in what ways?

I want you to **get a life**. I cannot do it for you. HECK! Some days I wonder if I have any influence with you. I want you to feel so loved and capable that you would not want to choose anything but good food for your body, start solving some of your problems and be available to your children as a healthy, supportive, caring and consistent parent.

Did you know?
Did you remember?
Today is my birthday.
I'm forty-eight years old.
Here I sit writing to my Kelly.
Because you are part of my story,
My life.
I count my blessings
And you are one of them.

I appreciated that you acknowledged my guess that you were **lost** again to the drug scene. Thanks for keeping open about what is and is not going on for you. I also liked that after you said you had lost our phone number and then corrected yourself by saying, "but I could have called information." Yes, you could have. So, I am interested in what stopped you. Still, I imagine, like not seeing the children, you did not call because your addiction stole you away, lost in time and thinking.

So, as ever, if you decide to come back to us, call, and we will talk about a plan to have you found, rediscovered, re-parented, re-birthed, renewed, re-cherished, reestablished and reconnected to your loved ones. Count me as a significant one.

About us: We had a Christmas Open House. Carl, a friend, played the piano while your Dad and Teeya played their guitars. At some point Ben came upstairs in a Santa suit and stole everyone's attention. I felt pleased with our tree this year. I decorated it in iced gingerbread cookies, taffeta bows, raffia, baby's breath and few pale blue balls—natural looking.

I created a whimsical angel display in one of the big plants in the living room with angel ornaments, snowflake doilies and twinkling, dainty lights. Delightful.

Katie goes to a wedding tomorrow and she will look stunning. Ben is seeing a young woman he says he would be pleased to marry, if she'd ever agree. Your dad and I continue enjoying our Sunday morning church going. Our Christmas newsletter (enclosed) tells of most of the other things you would find of interest.

My love, Mom

Kelly,
Merry Christmas and Happy New Year. The family loves and misses you. We are also afraid for you. Please find a safe direction before you get really hurt or into too much trouble.

Love, Ben

January 26, 1995
Calgary, Alberta

Dear Kelly

Thanks for calling last week from the London Detention Centre. I do not know what to think when we hear from you mostly from jail. I end up wanting you in jail more often. I like the contact.

You sounded happy that you will be caught up with charges and sentences. "Cleared" as you say. I'm glad you feel freer to talk about yourself, the internal turmoil you are going through and the hook alcohol and drugs have on you.

Enclosed is the information I said I would get about programs here. Riverside Villa has a twenty-eight day program and you would stay with us, attending the program in the day. Please consider taking a big step away from your chaos. I imagine that thinking about the possibilities is sometimes scary for you. You have potential. You are potential, your rhyming and writing, creativity, physical agility and caring nature.

You are not your experiences. You have experienced hooking, drugging, drinking, stabbing, nearly dying, giving birth, caring for your children, leaving your children, being beaten, being hugged and loved, losing your temper, stuffing your feelings, speaking encouragingly, cursing, eating your Mama's potato salad, starving, fist fighting, stealing, supporting, learning, vegging, stimulating your brain, damaging your brain, neglecting your brain, remembering your past, denying and ignoring your past.

But, you are you. You can choose the experiences. Please let us help and support you when you want to go toward health, clarity, care, love, encouragement and a life balanced with personal freedom and responsibility. Liberate yourself so that you have a meaningful place on this earth.

My love, Mom

February 8, 1995
Calgary, Alberta

Dear Kelly

You called on Sunday and I missed it. I missed you! Your Dad said that you seemed pleased to be out of jail and have been out for two weeks. Yet, you have not seen Danielle and James. He was impressed that you had not been drinking for many days. So, did I get the correct information?

Exciting news for me, is that I had a job interview for a two month contract with Alberta Alcohol and Drug Addiction Commission (AADAC). Wouldn't that be interesting? You could be a big help to me. You could be my consultant. What does the person challenged by alcohol and drugs need from helping professionals? What information do they need or want? How can I differentiate a truly motivated individual from one who is coming only because the court sent him or her?

I told the people interviewing me that I was interested in the position for personal and professional reasons. Mainly they want the person they hire to present mini workshops on various topics such as anger management, self-esteem, communication skills, problem solving, relapse prevention, healthy living and such. I would enjoy the work. I am quite sure. So, I'm waiting to hear back. I enjoy so many activities. I was off to an Integrated Body Psychotherapy weekend training when you called on the weekend.

Ben has bought himself a truck and is looking pleased. He will be paying monthly for goodness knows how long. Katie is kicking her feet up a bit since she finished exams. Some days when she fusses with herself, she looks so pretty. Your Dad works long hours and wonders how much longer he will be with the company.

Please phone again when I might be home.

Don't forget your invitation to have a break with us to get well.

Love, Mom

March 11, 1995
Calgary, Alberta

Dear Kelly

I called Lillian and she told me you were back in jail. When I called the jail they said the only way I could make contact, again, was to send a letter. Then all last night I was thinking of you. I will tell you more about that later.

Lillian also told me about her and the children's disappointment of not seeing you since Christmas day, when you visited them and stayed for some turkey. "Since Christmas!" I thought. James's sixth birthday was last week. My heart goes out to him and to you. He is missing the proud, caring, guiding eyes of his mother as he makes significant developmental leaps. Each day, week and month he is new, changed and growing. Kelly, you are missing the joy, challenge, responsibility and rewards of raising this wonderful little boy and, of course, Danielle.

Lillian said a stack of my letters to you is waiting at her place. I feel neglected. Then I think, "Me, a grown woman with lots of abundance, stimulation and caring people in my life feel neglected by Kelly." How neglected must Danielle and James feel? For more than ten years you have not acknowledged, even with a collect call, my birthday, Mother's Day, your Dad's or Ben's birthday, Katie's...and we miss the attention we'd like from you. Yet we have so much.

Of course I sent James a card, a couple of silly little things and some money. I am his Grandma but not his mother. Only you can do MOTHER things. James and Danielle have been greatly robbed by you, dear, and my heart aches some days. Can you tell I am feeling frustrated?

I worry. I expect your children, my grandchildren, are feeling highly abandoned. Just like you want to understand why your biological mother gave up, they must be wondering. Maybe your biological mother gave up on believing in herself. You seem to have given up on yourself. I hope not, totally.

Last night your Dad and I heard the story of a dear friend who had lost himself and now is found. I thought of you all last night. Bob is a recovered alcoholic and he was the speaker at an open AA meeting last night. Your Dad and I were invited to go with him. He even picked us up.

Bob has been sober for seventeen years. He talked about the days when he felt inferior and used booze as an equalizer. Then he told how he required a drink to steady himself. Then he had to find stronger and stronger alcohol to give him the same effect. Bob said to be hooked by an addiction was like riding a garbage truck. It was up to him to get off and the longer he stayed on, the closer and closer he came to arriving at the dump.

He told about some of his dead drinking buddies. He told about his wife, my friend, threatening to leave him with their children. He told about losing jobs, friends, and thousands of dollars. He told about AA saving his life, his marriage and his relationship with his children. And giving him FREEDOM to choose from the many options of a sober life. All night I thought of you.

Bob is not well-educated. My goodness, he hated school even more than you, I think. He lied about his age and began working for the railroad at age thirteen years. That is when he began his drinking. He was robbed of many, so-called, normal experiences in his adolescent years—as have you. Yet he now has a great bond with his nineteen-year-old daughter and twenty-year-old son, and a mutually nurturing marriage. In his seventeen years in AA, he repeatedly re-committed himself to staying off that garbage truck trip. All night I thought of you.

I have told Bob a bit about you and asked for his advice about how I could be a better help to you. I was given some pamphlets at the meeting. I expect you have seen them before but I wanted you to know that all night I thought of you.

I told Bob that you once said you were not going to promise to stay sober and clean because you get down on yourself and things seem to worsen for you. He said he used to use that excuse. He called it excuse number three. He believes that once you solemnly promise sobriety to a higher power, to your loved ones and yourself, that a difference will happen. Of course, you will not make perfect decisions, and you can re-commit. Of course Bob and I cannot decide anything for you, and all night I thought of you.

I started a new job this past Monday. I facilitate half-time in an employment training program for people who are on social assistance. I love the work. I talk about self-awareness, communication skills, assertiveness, self-esteem and stress management. My days are busy because I still do some counselling at Cambyr Agencies and do some volunteer work for a women's shelter. Next month I am presenting a workshop on self-esteem for some Islamic women. It should be interesting.

This afternoon, Katie and I are going out shopping for a grad dress. Ya! She is graduating from high school. She's already been accepted at the University of Calgary. She loves chemistry. Go figure? She sure is her Dad's girl.

She and I get along so much better. She is really moving out of that snotty teenager stage and is taking more responsibility for herself. She does very little complaining anymore that I make her life a total misery. She is maturing.

Ben is still sending out resumes. He is easy to live with. He sent you a note saying how worried he is about you. I expect it is with my letters at Lillian's.

Your Dad continues at work and is planning two or three canoe and camping trips for the spring and summer. He and I are on the Banff Couples Conference organizing committee so we spend time with other couples who are actively paying positive attention to their marriage.

We, of course, are wondering what happened to bring you back to jail. Remember, we feel, sometimes discouraged, sometimes frustrated, by the way you choose to live BUT we love and care about you. We want to know that you know we love you and want to help you.

We adopted you. We chose you. We decided to love and raise you and you were special and dear to us. All this is still true. Please call collect or write.

My love to you, Mom

March 12, 1995
Calgary, Alberta

Dear Kelly

I just hung up the phone with you. THANK YOU for calling. You weigh one hundred and fourteen pounds? Please eat! This is YOUR mother talking.

You are in jail over an unpaid fine? I do not understand all your jail visits.

I was glad to hear that you mailed James a birthday card from jail and called him on his special day. Tell me, if you were still partying, rather than in jail, would you have remembered his birthday? That's a curiosity question. I want to understand you better.

I feel discouraged that jail is where you seem to be the healthiest. I end up wanting you in jail as you seem better off, eating better, calling us and talking dearly. Then I feel guilty for wanting you in jail. Please find some places in the world where you can be safe, healthy and, eventually, happy most days.

Thank you so much for saying "I love you" before you hung up.

I love you, too, Mom

May 22, 1995
Calgary, Alberta

My dear Kelly

   Thank you for calling this morning to let me know you were in and out of the hospital. You went in Saturday, were operated on Sunday and out Monday morning. You must have had quite the fall. Were the stairs concrete to have smashed your face in like that? I cannot imagine a slit in your head and some instrument going down to reach your cheek bones and lifting them up. I feel shaky inside trying to imagine. Then you get out of your hospital bed so quickly. Your high pain threshold kicked in again, I bet.

   I was missing you. I had not heard from you since early March. Two months feels like a long time when I do not know whether you are well or even alive. I worry.

   I worry less when you stay connected. When I do not hear from you, I imagine that you are dead, feeling lost from us or drowned in your addictions.

   Terry, your older companion and alcoholic friend, sounds like a gentle guy. He talks as if he really cares about you. I was also so glad to hear that you saw James and Danielle on Friday. They need you, dear. You know that.

   Please get my letters from Lillian.

   I worry that the drugs and alcohol are sapping away your bright intellect, your health and your life energy. I was comforted to hear that you are eating real food and trying to cut back on your drug and alcohol consumption.

   I know you are struggling with an addiction, dear, and that your doubts about your lovableness and worthiness make going straight even harder. I know it, but of course, I do not really know the pain and depth of the despair you must live. I only imagine and I grieve the years of health and aliveness that your addictions have robbed from you. I grieve the Mommy your children love so sweetly, disappearing from their lives.

   Some days when I am thinking of you and my heart aches and leans in the direction of London, Ontario and you, I feel so HELPLESS to make a difference in your life.

I know your behaviour and choices are not my problem, not my issue, not my concern. They are yours. I just hope I have some influence with my hope and encouragement for you to face your insecurities and addictions and create a full life.

Please take care my dear, sweet girl.

Love, Mom

June 25, 1995
Calgary, Alberta

My dear Kelly

Your Dad and I went to a wedding today. What a wonderful experience. It was Neil's third marriage and I cannot imagine anything but this is now his time to be married successfully to the right person for him. I cried. The beautiful words of commitment were taken from a book called **Illuminata** by Marianne Williamson, a spiritual teacher.

As you can see, enclosed is a letter I wrote in May. It was sent back to me twice. Here I am trying to meet you again.

I was telling a close—spiritually aware—friend about my struggle to keep my feelings of hope about your future. She asked me an interesting question, "Hope for what, Pat?" I replied with my usual conviction and determination. I told her what I hope is that one day you will declare battle against your addictions and create health, purpose and renewed relationships with yourself, your children, family and me.

After talking to her, I decided that I want more to unconditionally, simply and truly love and acknowledge you, Kelly for you, the beautiful, lovable, creative, powerful you, AS IS. I love you as you are.

I think of all you have taught me. You have shared your struggle with life, the truth of your addiction and your true feelings. I have learned so much by you doing things so differently than I would wish. No matter how much energy I put into wanting to steer it in other directions, you do life your way. What a lesson for me. I am slowly really understanding that I need to orchestrate my own life. Thank you, dear.

Ben is still so in love with his woman friend. He is home right now as he is going on a four day canoe trip with your Dad. He has begun to keep a journal, like a diary, in the most splendid and creative way— jotting feelings, observations, wonderings and adding a sketch now and then. Katie has a young man with whom she is spending time. She met him through the Internet, a computer-created relationship.

Sure hope this gets to you. Please pick up your mail from Lillian's and see the children. Oops, there I go again.

My love, Mom

July 2, 1995
Calgary, Alberta

Dear Kelly,

I felt so happy after you called this morning from jail. Your voice was like music to my ears. I am so glad you finally know, get and believe that we do love you. I feel very hopeful for you, dear. You sounded so bright, happy and healthy—almost, as if jail was a kind of heaven. You talked about reading in church, participating in art class, making a rug, going to AA meetings, enjoying talks on women's awareness and reading the thick **Kane and Abel** novel in two days. You also said that you liked waking up without a hangover and phoning the kids every day. I feel encouraged by the way you are thinking about your future. You have even thought of the advantages of going on welfare.

I could picture you when you described one experience: "One day I was watching the birds and thinking about something I had done for someone. I thought, 'Jees!, I usually do things like that in those kind of situations.' I felt a quiet happiness. Then I had a couple of days of loving myself. I thought, 'I don't even want a beer'." You acknowledged that this was the first time you remember having loving thoughts and feelings towards yourself. I feel so excited for you. It sounds like you are developing an accepting and caring relationship with yourself.

For years I have been working at revealing unconscious parts of myself, like peeling an onion, and then experimenting with accepting and loving that new discovered part. Welcome to personal growth. What a wonderful step in healing yourself. The more you can feel what you feel without judging, the more you can love yourself. You will feel that "quiet happy" you talked about, inside yourself. Then you can do it for your kids and others. As I said Kelly, when you make a difference for you, you make a difference for many people.

It sounded like you made a difference in the jail when you declared your love for me. "I love my mom!" Wow! Right in the jail. I feel honoured by my gutsy gal of a daughter. Then some other girls "got the guts to say the same thing" about their mothers. Your guts are contagious. When you claim your truth, you are a powerful woman. You described stopping a beating-up of Tommy's new girlfriend in the jail, "to keep peace in the family." Whatever the reason, you chose kindness for those involved. I feel so proud of you.

I do encourage you to write down any flashbacks or memories that come up for you. Yes, you will feel some pain, but this time you will be seeing the situation from an adult's perspective. You will know that it was the offending adult who was violating you. When you were a kid, you felt the pain and probably believed it was because you were bad. That is simply not the truth. I imagine your addictions have been drowning your memories and pain. They have also drowned the peaceful, loving feelings and the truth that you were an innocent, dependent child. You were told a bunch of lies and experienced unjust pain and rejection. The truth is you are lovable just as you are...and capable, too.

Things that matter the most must not be at the mercy of things that matter the least.

Kelly matters the most right this moment.

Here is a bit of news from us. Katie is feeling frustrated about not hearing yet from McMaster University about acceptance. She has signed up and paid for her science courses at the University of Calgary so there is no doubt about her attending university. However, McMaster remains her preferred option.

She has been hired by the Calgary Stampede and Exhibition Board for four hours of balloon twisting in Kiddy Land for all ten days of Stampede. She is excellent at twisting these balloons. Who would have ever guessed that when she started this at age ten, she would be making some decent money at it? She continues to be the Balloon Lady at Pizza Hut Tuesday nights and does birthday parties as Sassy, the clown, once in a while. She has her first boyfriend, so tentative and sweet. Dennis is a few months younger than her.

Ben has an interview next week for a permanent position as an EMT in a community just south of Edmonton. He has also been short listed for the Calgary Police Department so will be writing an aptitude exam for that sometime this month. Nine hundred and ninety-nine people and Ben will write the first round of tests. His amoured eyes still look toward Chandra, a wonderful elementary school teacher.

Your dad goes to work, putting in time, it seems. He's glad to have a job and, yet, ready to feel glad to be laid off, whenever. Then, we would probably move back to Ontario. I want Danielle and James to spend weekends and some summer holidays with us. You too, of course. Your Dad bought himself a second canoe for doing solo canoeing. He saw a deal in the local **Bargain Finder**. It is classic, red painted wood and fourteen feet long—three feet shorter than his other canoe. I love to see him treat himself. It takes the guilt feeling away that I sometimes have when I see him work such long hours while I travel through life with freedom of choice of how I spend my time and energy.

That time and energy? Recently I co-wrote a proposal for provincial funds to open and operate family resource centres in Calgary. I am counselling individuals and couples at Cambyr Agencies. Since Ben moved out, I am counselling people at the house in his old bedroom. I attend my Toastmaster club each week, sometimes giving a speech. I still facilitate parent education courses and workshops for the Catholic School Board. As a volunteer service, I provide counselling at a women's shelter and I am organizing my church's summer picnic. Do you remember how I used to organize family parties at the Sarnia Riding Club? What fun.

I am feeling hormonally challenged many days and I do not like it. I usually use humour to deal with my loss of memory, energy and sleep. I am a CHANGED woman alright!

Your Uncle John, Mary Jane, Reilly and Kaitlin are arriving this Friday from Edmonton to participate in Stampede with us. Your Uncle Peter will be here for a 2 week holiday. My, my, my, such a busy and full life.

Just this last week Ben came home from High Prairie (he works as a casual Emergency Medical Technician) so that he and Les could go on a long weekend canoe and camping trip with a dozen other guys. Ben made the most funny and loving card for your dad on Father's Day. What a guy. I bet you two could have some neat times together. Ben plays so delightfully and he makes wonderful contact with children.

I am flying to Ontario on July 14 and sometime after that I will come to London. You are definitely on my want to see list so I will visit the London Middlesex Detention Centre. Perhaps I could arrange with Lillian to bring the children with me. How would that be? Most of my time, however, will be spent with your grandma in Fenelon Falls.

I will send this package of photos and notes off to you and trust that it will get to you. Know that I love you and keep you in my thoughts and heart. See you soon, dear.

Love, Mom

# 4
## ...the miracle "yes"

M Y HOLIDAY TO ONTARIO BEGAN WHEN I STEPPED OUTSIDE the airport terminal and right into the wall of a sticky Toronto heat wave. July 18, 1995 was the day I drove west on the 401—in my friend Sandra's car—from Toronto down to London. Along the way I remember seeing a billboard that read "Worry is interest paid on trouble before it is due." I thought, "Not necessarily true in respect to Kelly." Many of my worried imaginings had taken form, but I had learned to minimize the energy I put into worrying. After picking up five-year-old James and four-year-old Danielle from their grandmother's apartment, I found my way to the Elgin-Middlesex Detention Centre.

The children and I were required to pass through a front door security check before entering a room that felt like a cellar, constructed as is was with an outer wall of concrete blocks and an inner chamber with walls of thick glass. Other than the colour of concrete, the space was completely white. We sat on round stools—like stumps of wood—secured to the floor, with a glass wall and telephones in front of us. Kelly could talk to us only through a telephone. The hard countertop reverberated loudly when I accidentally dropped my car keys. The whole environment was cold, hard, crude and archaic.

When Kelly walked through the doors into her glassed cage, she grinned broadly and walked toward us with a saucy swagger. She wore baggy sweat pants, a tee shirt and slippers on her lean body. Certainly the look was different than her usual tight jeans and black leather jacket combo. She waved, and blew kisses, and put two phones to her head, one on each ear and pointed to the children to each pick one. The telephone handsets had very short cords which made talking, while perched on the stools, quite difficult. So many of this jail's visiting arrangements made a loving connection next to impossible. However, children manage in amazing ways. Some of the conversation between them and Kelly pierced my heart.

**Danielle**: I drew you a picture, Mom. When you get out of jail I'll give it to you. I wish you could get out now. That glass; maybe if we had a baseball bat we could hit it, smash it. I love you, Mom.

**Kelly**: I love you too, up to the stars and down to the grass.

**Danielle**: I'll write you a letter. I'll sing you the alphabet. Do you want to hear it? ABC...next time will you sing with me?

**Kelly**: Next time I will sing with you.

**James**: Put down that phone! You are under arrest. Remain silent.

**Danielle**: When you get out of jail I'm going to make you something. Maybe I'll live with you forever.

When it was my turn to connect through the phone she was so light and cheerful — such a contradiction to the hard and confining surroundings. I wanted to smash the thick, smudged and scratched glass just as Danielle had expressed. But then what? I had played with a number of words to express my concern. "What did I have left that I hadn't already expressed in letters?" I asked myself. "Should I just play it straight? Scream? Declare that we all have had enough of this crazy life? Didn't she know what it was doing to the children and us? Stay loving?" I decided to ask a simple and caring question. Somewhere in the middle of the noise, the love talk, James playing with his car on the cold cement, the echoing of our voices, and the passing of phones back and forth I managed to ask, "Are you ready to go into treatment, dear?" My breathing stopped. A defined space in time existed. I felt stunned at the answer that was, "Yes, Mom." Much was arranged and has happened since those two words were spoken.

# 5
# ...Kelly fills in the gaps

I N THE FOLLOWING INTERVIEW, KELLY DESCRIBES HER PERSPECTIVE of her childhood and her very turbulent, addicted years, how she became involved with drugs, what she believed and how she managed her life. This mother-daughter exchange took courage for both of us. I needed to breathe consciously and really listen without judging her or defending myself. I found these stories saddening, frightening, troubling, sometimes confusing and a relief to hear. The truth sounded true. Thank goodness I had made myself safe enough for her to self-disclose. Thank goodness she was able to separate who I was from the mother I used to be. The foggy window of Kelly, who she is, where she had been, and what she had done, became clearer.

Kelly revealed her warrior woman as well as her vulnerable, scared inner child while clearly and openly filling the gaps of her life. To share these dark and long-kept secret places with me was an enormous leap of faith. I noticed that her vocabulary and tone of voice assumed a tough ambiance as she remembered and talked about her participation with alcohol, drugs, and incarceration. It took incredible trust in my continued love of her to do the telling. Our relationship experienced, yet another, healing.

This conversation took place in the summer of 1996, one year after Kelly had entered the recovery process.

**Patricia**: OK if we start with your childhood? Your first memories are probably in the foster home.

**Kelly**: I hadn't and haven't slept through the night for years. The foster mother used to come in at night to check if I was asleep and if I wasn't she'd give me a beating with a wooden spoon. I used to pretend I was asleep, but it didn't work. It doesn't bother me now because I've been over it so often.

**Patricia**: Were there other times?

**Kelly**: I broke something when I was supposed to stand still for a picture and when I didn't I got hit. In her house you could run around the organ and I broke a vase. Miss DuMoulin (adoption social worker) was the only one who treated me specially. I wish she had adopted me. When I was with her, I was the focus. Other places, I was never first. I was never the baby in any family. Georgia, another foster child, was like a sister. She was a little younger than me. I remember seeing her go away in a car. I remember crying. Only as an adult do I understand what happened. She was adopted and I was left behind.

**Patricia**: I gather you don't remember what happened with the first family that adopted you. I do know now that you felt ripped off when I told you that our house looked like a ginger bread house. I really thought it did, Kelly. I was so proud of our first home.

**Kelly**: Ya. I was really mad. Now I can understand. But you told a little kid who didn't have anything that she was moving into a ginger bread house. I thought, "Now the Gods are finally smiling on me." I remember Dad, but when I was little, my family really consisted of you and Ben. I knew you were interested in me. I didn't know Dad. You said I was scared of men. Didn't you say when I first saw him I was scared?

**Patricia**: We were told you were scared of men. It was in your documentation that your mother was with a live-in man and each time a man walked into the room you would scream.

**Kelly**: This is what I need to know. She got pregnant in the States. Did she get me back or what happened?

**Patricia**: We were told you went back and forth from her to foster homes several times.

**Kelly**: Did they take me or did she willingly give me up?

**Patricia**: We weren't told.

**Kelly**: Well, I want to know that.

**Patricia**: I bet you do. Why the back and forth, we don't know. We were given just bits of information.

**Kelly**: I've always been afraid of men. I was so jealous of Ben. I resented him and thought, "I just got here and he's the baby." I thought, "I hate the little bugger" and he looked like you guys. I felt like an alien.

**Patricia**: That's understandable. Because you were adopted as the youngest the first time and that adoption did not work out, the theory was that this time you would be the oldest. What would your life have been like if we had adopted you when Ben and Katie were older?

**Kelly**: Wouldn't life have been different? My God, yes!

**Patricia**: Can you say more?

**Kelly**: When I got older, say eleven, twelve or thirteen I thought you adopted me to show off to your friends, to show how you could take a poor little rejected kid and turn her into this magnificent thing. I thought that was why you were bending me so hard to be what you wanted me to be. That was very damaging because no one ever let me be who I wanted to be since the day I was born.

**Patricia**: With all that energy, your mother, your father, no counsellors, or teachers said, "Isn't she wonderful?" We all let you down. You are energetic. You are spontaneous and more than that.

**Kelly**: You're a good Mom for me now. Who on this planet could mother me better than you do?

**Patricia**: If only I had learned my lessons earlier.

**Kelly**: Me too.

**Patricia**: All the "if only"s. And if only I had got saner sooner and we all had clued in to your Attention Deficit condition.

**Kelly**: That's easy to say and I say it too, but I still have a lot of anger. I have so much anger because I had so many people tell me that I was bad.

**Patricia**: Of course, you'd feel angry. The question that was asked was, "Why isn't anyone able to discipline this child?"

**Kelly**: But I'm not going to harp on it for the rest of your life. My feelings were all shoved down.

**Patricia**: Clamped and no one saw that.

**Kelly**: One person did, Mickey Sloot (therapist). He gave the message, "Honour your impulsiveness. Honour your creativity. Honour your energy."

**Patricia**: So, he was ahead of everyone else.

**Kelly**: Way ahead without excusing me. He didn't excuse my behaviour at all. All the rest of my world was focusing on the bad things I had done. I couldn't wait to tell him. He'd listen and say, "You're still OK." Murray Jackson at ALPS (Alternative Learning Program) was like that, too.

**Patricia**: I'm glad you had these guys caring for you. Interesting that you say you are afraid of men yet the two people you could talk to were men.

**Kelly**: They earned my trust. You lost my trust. It was horrible. I remember sitting on my bed and I was getting ready to go to camp. I put on purple shorts and a red shirt and you said something like, "Take that off." And I thought I looked so pretty and mature dressing myself. You said, "Take it off. It looks horrible together," and you took out all my clothes and put them together. You asked, "Do you see that,

that looks horrible?" In my head I was thinking, "That looks beautiful," and out of my mouth I'm saying, "I see that looks horrible."

**Patricia**: So I really taught you not to be truthful.

**Kelly**: And not to trust my judgement.

**Patricia**: You know how I've told you, "I've tended to be such a goodie-two-shoes in the world and follow what I thought were the rules?" I'm sorry.

**Kelly**: I know. You didn't want people to see your daughter in mismatched clothes.

**Patricia**: You've got it.

**Kelly**: I struggle with Danielle when she wants to go out the door in something that looks out to lunch. I always felt that if I could get past a shield you had up that life would be better.

I remember you reading *Cat in the Hat* curled upstairs on pillows in bed. But my favourite book, *The Eye Book*, has a part I really liked. "Our eyes see flies. Our eyes see ants. Sometimes they see pink underpants." I remember when you read to me about how babies are made at the little table in the living room and I was sitting in my little chair. You were sitting in your little chair and that was so sweet. I remember you reading me stories but usually I was in shit from one direction or another. So, that was hard for you.

**Patricia**: And you. How was elementary school?

**Kelly**: It was hard because it was boring and I just wanted to liven it up, which caused trouble. I was bored!

**Patricia**: Was it like what that book on ADD described as time being warped into very long or very short depending on your interest?

**Kelly**: Long? When I was kid I didn't have control or Ritalin like I do now. When you have ADD and you are at your boredom limit you feel a big explosion. It is like someone lights a fire under you and you'll get burned if you sit there.

**Patricia**: That's why you ended up doing somersaults in the school hallways.

**Kelly**: Oh, ya. Here's where it sucked. I never put the consequence together. Ah, it still bothers me. I'd leave the class thinking, "Oh, I screwed up a little bit," and dance the rest of the way home. I wouldn't expect that in a couple of days you would be devastated when you found out about it. I remember in England the teacher called you. I thought, "I haven't been too good or too bad." I didn't see anything horrible I had done. I waited outside the school by the portable. I waited until all the kids and teachers had gone home. I got home late that day because I stopped the teacher and pleaded and begged and begged to not to get you upset. Well she blew it. Maybe that's what set you off in England.

**Patricia**: Yes, that could have been the time. Actually, I think I heard five months of what was going on — different stories than you told me. When you were kept in for detentions you would tell me you were helping or volunteering.

**Kelly**: Yup. You don't know how awful I felt waiting. How many interviews did you go to?

**Patricia**: Not many. Of course in England the schools are stricter which would have made it harder on you. That teacher had a lot of problems with you and I definitely was not a help.

**Kelly**: Stricter! Mom? In front of the class the teacher told me I was just like those dirty Americans. They all laughed at me.

**Patricia**: Oh, no! Kelly.

**Kelly**: We're like two years behind them academically so I was considered stupid. I was stupid. I had an accent. The kids taunted and teased me. The teacher said, "Ok, everybody, put on your pumps. We're going out to the playground." I thought pumps were pogos that you bounce on so I was all excited. Pumps were plain old running shoes. The kids all laughed at me, called me an idiot and were pushing me off the swing.

**Patricia**: So, I was pregnant, depressed, angry or both while school was awful for you.

**Kelly**: I had nothing to live for. I didn't even have a husband to comfort me or a grandma or anyone. Six months to a kid feels like years.

**Patricia**: So England was a big black hole for you. I didn't know you were taunted and teased.

**Kelly**: I remember one fun thing in England. When you and I couldn't figure out how to do up my tie on my school uniform. We wound up laughing and you said, "To hell with it, let's go."

**Patricia**: Were there any particularly happy times?

**Kelly**: I was going to say when we went to Disney Land in Florida but you guys freaked on me there. We were all in a hotel room and I couldn't sleep, as usual. I tried to stay so still. Do you see how damaging the ADD can be?

**Patricia**: Misunderstood and frustrating, huh? How was life for you at the Sarnia Riding Club? We joined that family club because I just couldn't keep up with you after Katie was born.

**Kelly**: I had a lot of fun with the other girls. Cindy, the coach, was great. It gave me time away from you in a healthy environment. Remember when I did a back dive, whacked my leg on the board and had a huge bruise? I was so proud I could finally do a back dive. I said, "Mom watch." Then you watched and I went wham, hitting the board before going into the water.

**Patricia**: Ah. Gymnastics was a wonderful sport for you and we felt dreadful taking you out.

**Kelly**: I could have been a pro but I couldn't focus enough. I wish we had known about ADD and Ritalin back then. I couldn't learn a strict routine. I was impulsive and changed my routine, which worked well once when I won a gold medal for something I made up on bars. I was so excited to get on the bars. I couldn't wait my turn. I thought I would die waiting.

**Patricia**: So it was hard to contain yourself and then you had the disappointment of the gymnastics curtailed.

**Kelly**: I'm not resentful about that, at all, Mom. They were right. I was disruptive. That had to be done.

**Patricia**: Oh, I'm glad to hear that. Gymnastics was important to you. Do you remember giving classes in the back garden to Katie and the neighbourhood kids?

**Kelly**: Ya. The gym was my haven. I was so used to failures in my life. I never had successes until I went into recovery. What did I succeed at? I almost got kicked out of Outboard Bound.

**Patricia**: What happened?

**Kelly**: My behaviour was mostly good there. I made friends with Wendy and Laura Lee.

**Patricia**: What do you mean, "You almost got kicked out?"

**Kelly**: For smoking in the forest. That's good for me. I got piss drunk on the island during the survival part.

**Patricia**: How did you get the alcohol? You're creative!

**Kelly**: We were a hundred miles north of Thunder Bay and they put us each on an island for forty-eight hours. We were in the boonies. You forget. There are natives there. You get about three matches, a bag of trail mix and a sleeping bag. No tent. Some natives were fishing in a little dinky aluminum fishing boat. They were really drunk. Who would imagine way up there. I called them, "Hey! Come on over!" We partied. When the Outward Bound leaders came to get me the next day there were empty beer bottles all over my little island. Me and all these drunk Indians were passed out. The leaders were mad. It was a big secret. The other girls weren't told about it. I think they were worried about getting sued.

**Patricia**: We thought we sent you on a wholesome experience. The letter that described your participation did talk about a "rebellious nature." What do you remember about your time at the children's residential home?

**Kelly**: I had to stand in a corner, with my hands on my head for, it seemed, hours. Because of my small bladder it seemed longer. A child that age would do anything not to pee in front of males. There were no other girls there at the time. It was all boys. I remember the pee trickling down my legs and I was so ashamed. It was like I broke into little pieces...and then I puked. I was so dizzy. I think they made me wipe it up.

I didn't have any dolls there. You had given me some bubble bath in a plastic, doll shaped bottle. When the bubble bath was used up I slept with the bottle. One staff came in. She was so nice and had long, long hair like Miss DuMoulin. The next day she brought me in a stuffed doggie, Pierre, with red hair and a funny hat. She gently took away the plastic bottle.

**Patricia**: Ah! You couldn't take any of your dolls from home there?

**Kelly**: I don't remember. Most of the staff were mean to me. With their punishments I didn't get a fresh start each day. Is that any way to treat a kid? When you wake up you know you are on insight and dressed like an orphan. That kind of shame and humiliation does not put you in a position to reach for the stars. I always knew that you loved me with cuddles and you told me but I always felt like I was bad. I was pretty happy when I started hanging out with Chris and we smoked dope.

**Patricia**: We had no idea you were using drugs at the age of thirteen. How did that get started?

**Kelly**: I started to smoke weed (Refer to Appendix II) at thirteen. Chris and I got eight joints, I think for five dollars, from her brother. Chris and I were so high we left the roaches in a bag on the kitchen table. Luanne found them and said nothing to me. She gave them to Dad. I was so mad at Luanne. I was more relieved Dad didn't notice we drank his booze. I had mixed some horrible drinks. They were disgusting. You came to me and said, "What are these?" I said, "We were at Chris'. Her brother was smoking dope and made her get them out of the house." Then you said, "I knew they weren't yours."

**Patricia**: I sure was unaware. You progressed from weed to acid? We didn't know anything about it and were so naive. Did the drug use interfere with school?

**Kelly**: So, so. I didn't really go to school. Then when I was sixteen I left home. I ran away twice before to other cities.

**Patricia**: Was it more like exploring on your part? It did not feel, from our perspective, like you were totally running away.

**Kelly**: Well, that was the intention (laugh).

**Patricia**: Unbeknown to us. So fill me in about what was happening.

**Kelly**: It sucked at home.

**Patricia**: So, it sucked at home and it sucked at school.

**Kelly**: It was boring and a drag.

**Patricia**: Finally you decided to get out. You took off with a friend. So what happened?

**Kelly**: We went to this place, a town, way up north. I was going out with a guy who liked me a lot. Rodney was really nice but I was so bored all the time. I'd grab him and hitchhike to Toronto and all over. Finally, he got sick of the traveling (laugh).

**Patricia**: So you lived at his place.

**Kelly**: With his mom. We just partied.

**Patricia**: Mom, too?

**Kelly**: No. She was old. I remember we just went around town partying. After I lived with Chris' family for awhile, I had an apartment with Terry in Sarnia. We used to party.

**Patricia**: What does the term "party" mean?

**Kelly**: We party. Get in trouble with the law.

**Patricia**: Does it mean using drugs, staying up all night and maybe several days?

**Kelly**: Ya. Somehow I ended up in Kitchener with my friend, Karen. Her boyfriend and I lived in the bike gang's club house. None of them live there.

**Patricia**: You stayed there, cleaned, looked after the toilets and things?

**Kelly**: No! We had the top apartment. A guy I knew back then, Doug, we got along really well and I bumped into him years later in London and he has his own paving company. He said, "Whoa. You were a tiny little girl." I lived there for about six months.

**Patricia**: How would you eat and survive?

**Kelly**: We stole from the market. Man! We were high. We weren't hungry. That's when I really started drugs — big time. They let me drink but I was only sixteen so they wouldn't let me do coke. We would take kilograms of hash and gold seal stamp it.

**Patricia**: What does "gold seal" mean?

**Kelly**: Gold seal is a kind of hash. If there's a gold seal on it, it is good hash. We had kilogram bricks of it. We were stamping it to sell it.

**Patricia**: To sell? So you would be working for the club in exchange for the room?

**Kelly**: No. I'd just be around.

**Patricia**: How did you wing this deal of staying there?

**Kelly**: Just because I was Karen's friend. Her boyfriend was in the gang. We didn't have to pay a cent.

**Patricia**: They did not let you use coke, but you could use hash.

**Kelly**: Oh, ya and acid. I got lost on a set of stairs, once. I was too high. I could not figure out how to get off these stairs. We laughed for hours and hours (laugh). Oh, ya! We had a lot of fun.

**Patricia**: What did you do for clothes?

**Kelly**: Stole them.

**Patricia**: So, you stole food and clothes. There was nothing else you really needed — basic living in some ways? How did you end up leaving?

**Kelly**: I met Art through Karen and moved in with him. Drink! Oh, my God. His mom was an alcoholic. We used to smoke, too. His mom's boyfriend had an old van parked in the driveway. Me, Art, Johnny and Steve—we'd go out with big hunks of hash with a torch and do hot knives in the van. We'd be fried every day.

**Patricia**: Explain what you would do with hot knives.

**Kelly**: When they're red hot you put the hash in little teeny balls and touch it. The hot knife picks up the hash and it sticks on the other red hot one. You smoke it with a toilet paper roll. That's one way to smoke hash. We got high every single day. One of us always had dope. Art's brother dealt. That's when I got pregnant.

**Patricia**: That is when you took a different path for a month or so and resided in a home for pregnant teenagers.

**Kelly**: Yup. I was devastated when I had to have an operation. That really bummed me out because I moved into that home for pregnant girls and quit smoking drugs. I didn't touch anything.

**Patricia**: So it really felt like you had turned a corner.

**Kelly**: Ya. I really wanted to have a nice, healthy baby. I did try to go straight. I didn't have to go into that home. Then I got robbed. (Note: The pregnancy had to be aborted for a pre-cancer condition called hydatidiform mole.) So I said, "Fuck this."

**Patricia**: That was an effort on your part to turn things around only to have it not work out. You were seventeen, very young and pretty scared. I remember visiting you in the Kitchener hospital when you had the operation. You asked to come home. It was hard for me not to say "yes." I arranged for you to move to London, to the girls' home, Belton House, as a transition or try out. Then, I said, "We'll talk about coming home."

**Kelly**: Brenda Hall was director at Belton House who I knew from the group home. I was there and met my best friend Annette. We smoked dope every single day. Once we went out to smoke dope at Labatts Park, across the street. We were on acid already and we went to smoke some weed. Another girl that we had taken acid with, who was so high, went up and tried to play checkers with the staff. She was so high that she got caught, squealed on us and shut the door so we got locked out smoking dope in the park. Warren, one of the staff, stuck his head out and said, "Girls!" That Vicky! I punched her every time I saw her after that.

**Patricia**: Literally, punched her?

**Kelly**: Ya! So me and Annette said, "We don't care anyways. Bye!" And I think we left that night. Then the fun began. We hitchhiked out west. Annette and I got in a fight so I left her in the Okanogan Valley.

**Patricia**: You sent us a photograph from there. So you hitchhiked across the country with nothing but the clothes on your back. Did you steal, again, to eat?

**Kelly**: No. People gave us money. I came back with more money than I had.

**Patricia**: People like, who?

**Kelly**: Truck drivers, and not for sex, either. We got high all the way there and back.

**Patricia**: So there are truck drivers that are good guys?

**Kelly**: Lots!

**Patricia**: Did any of them ask for sex?

**Kelly**: Maybe, like one. Most of them were protective and called us "kids." "Did you kids eat?" "Do your parents know where you are?" and "Don't tell me you kids are twenty." They would say, "I have a daughter your age." We'd lie and say we had money but they'd give us ten bucks and say, "Stick it in your pocket anyway." They'd buy us meals. One of us would sleep and the other would stay awake. We always did that.

**Patricia**: Protection from rape?

**Kelly**: Ya. Once we were hitchhiking to Toronto. We were stuck on the 401. It was really blocked. I got in the front. Annette got in the back. She went to sleep. The guy started to grab me. I started punching on him. I said, "Annette, come on," and I jumped right out.

**Patricia**: Annette was a friend that provided protection. Have you kept in touch with her?

**Kelly**: Annette is the most mellow person, a little, sweet hippy. She's got multiple sclerosis now. She was at University of Waterloo, I think. She never was like me. She was always hippy, free and full of peace and love. Wouldn't fight for anything. She introduced me to a girl named Deeda who's like my twin—looks like me, talks like me. Everybody in London would say, "You remind me of Deeda." I asked Annette, "Who's this Deeda?" She introduced me and we got along great. Deeda's boyfriend, Mike George, talks like that (W.C. Fields) weird guy. Mike George is dead now. That's when I started to use speed.

When I was seventeen a whole bunch of us—me, Mike, Deeda, George, Annette—a whole clan of us—we'd go to the Western Fair and sit right outside the arcade. I'd cut up pieces of paper and sell it for acid—four dollars a hit.

**Patricia**: You had acid on you?

**Kelly**: No. It was only cut up paper. I'd pour black paint in a vial and boom sell it as hash oil. Sold!

**Patricia**: You were a professional con? When did you learn to pull con jobs?

**Kelly**: We just learned. You gotta eat. You gotta buy your drugs.

**Patricia**: They introduced you to speed.

**Kelly**: Ya. But before that I had been stealing ten to fifteen cases of beer from Labatts at a time, in a van. I was taking my friends in there on Sundays and giving them tours around Labatts.

**Patricia**: In the factory? You knew how to get in?

**Kelly**: I could tell you where the Schooner, the Blue, the Blue Light was. I could climb those cases right up, pull the plastic off and pull one up. There are fences up now. I had a line-up of bums from the Salvation Army, a big brigade from the Salvation Army from across the street. We were passing case after case right across the street piling them up by some bushes. We must have had twenty-five or thirty cases before someone called the cops. All these old hobos and bums (laugh) and I was the director (laugh). All these old guys who live at the Salvation Army were in heaven, so happy and yelling.

Annette and I moved in a couple of blocks from there with a guy called Darren. There was a fence that I just fit through. Annette would pass the beer through to me. I took my friends in for a tour on Sunday. We went through the tunnels and went into the employee's lounge. I said, "Would you like a beer?" and we drank out of their little fridge. Then I said, "This concludes the tour of Labatts Beer" (laugh). Oh my God. I did that, for real.

Once I was stealing beer when I was pregnant with Danielle. I was eight months pregnant and with a guy, Steve, who had a very, very bad record. We had a car full of beer and a security guard caught us. Steve "bam" punched and knocked him out. No kidding, Mom. "Boom," the guy went down. We hopped into the car. Steve was going to run over him. I said, "No, don't run over him." The guy (the security guard) got our license number. They found the car and we got busted. But I was hiding under Steve's Mom—hiding under her couch. I was big, pregnant and squashed under that couch. All the beer was in the garage. We got charged for robbery and Steve smashed the security guard's jaw. I already did my time for it. Remember I was in jail pregnant. I got three months. Steve got eighteen months.

**Patricia**: So you met Deeda and then?

**Kelly**: Deeda's boyfriend was Mike and they had a street kid who was fourteen, called Mikey. Mikey's brother, Rick, used to be one of my best friends. I was the last person to see him alive. He committed suicide.

**Patricia**: You have had a number of friends die.

**Kelly**: Oh ya. Rick and Ronnie Allen. He got his head blown off in Kirkland Lake. Connie, a good friend, overdosed on heroin. She was nice. She worked at Bell Telephone. She was on methadone. Duke got blown away by my friend, Frank. Duke was my friend for twelve years. Before, Duke's wife, Gail, overdosed and Duke and his friends threw her out on the lawn so she'd look like she overdosed herself. Tommy and I were there that night. We were there the night Duke got shot. They had a little boy who was ten. He used to watch pornos, weighing up dope, throwing knives in the walls. I know a lot of ones that died.

**Patricia**: A lot of death. Have you been to funerals?

**Kelly**: Oh, ya. That's where they do half their deals, because everybody's there. It's all one clique. "Where you been? What'a ya got?"

**Patricia**: Trading and dealing?

**Kelly**: Kind of like a get to-gether. I was at my friend Ruth's funeral. She was good people. They said "natural causes"—heart attack—but she was my age. At her funeral they played Led Zeppelin just cranked. Ruth was well loved. Faith died of AIDS. Her mother got murdered in London, her head chopped off with an axe. Faith saw it and she was only eight. She and her sister were hiding in the closet. She saw her mother get decapitated with an axe. The guy who did it went to jail for twenty years.

**Patricia**: You lived in this whole different world. So you were living with Deeda now?

**Kelly**: We just hung around using alcohol and speed. I was stealing five cases of beer and selling them for fifty bucks, like ten bucks each. I'd get a half gram of speed. I made a killing off the beer. I made thousands of dollars off of Labatts. When I lived with Art, in Kitchener, I sold off his alcoholic Mom's wine. I was only sixteen. I was down at Oktoberfest selling bottles of wine. "Five bucks! Only five bucks!" Remember, I said, I can sell what I believe in, well, you should have seen me selling that wine. It went like hot cakes. I was selling off all her wine. She thought she was twice the alcoholic she was (laugh).

**Patricia:** So you met Tommy through Deeda.

**Kelly:** He was her dealer. He gave me the biggest hit of speed. I was so high. He wanted sex for the longest time and I said, "No." I was hanging out with my friend Karen and we moved in the nunnery. This place was nuts. It was an old nunnery with sixty, spooky rooms with a guy who had a lobotomy, all the rest were drug addicts. It was a great big drug house, that's all. Tommy started to sell his speed out of there. He'd pay a guy to sit in the bushes with a walkie talkie. He got the owner hooked.

**Patricia:** How did he do that?

**Kelly:** Just gave him some.

**Patricia:** Tell me a little bit about speed. I do not know anything about it.

**Kelly:** No. I don't want to think about it.

**Patricia:** OK. So tell me what happened.

**Kelly:** I caught Tommy and my friend, Karen, fooling around so I smashed a wine bottle and chased her with it. I robbed an A&M machine using a credit card that I got from stealing a purse. It had the woman's pin number right on the key. I'll never forget that. It makes me happy, even now thinking about it (the money coming out of the machine). That's terrible. I was smart. I sunk the purse in the river.

Tommy had got busted big time and was in jail for a few years— just before I met him. He didn't have anything until I stole that money. I gave him the money and he was off and running again. We lived in hotels dealing dope.

Later he went to jail and I started stripping. I stayed in the house and drank alcohol every single day. You go out to a hick town outside of London to strip dance. You do what you want. You learn. It was fun. I was drunk every day and I had money coming out of my...

**Patricia:** Can you strip when you are drunk?

**Kelly:** Ya. It's the only way you can.

**Patricia:** Are many of the girls hooked on drugs?

**Kelly:** Ninety percent.

**Patricia:** Do the people who hire them provide the drugs?

**Kelly:** Oh, no. They'd lose their license. A lot of bikers get their women stripping and have them in the bars selling it. This one girl, every night I went to work she'd say, "Here have a free toke of coke. I'd say, "No, I don't want it." The girls in there are selling for the dealers and they give you your first toke. Then you need it all night long. Then you owe them your whole week's check. If you do crack, if you do one toke, you're going to smoke all night long. You can't just do one. They figure, get that first one into you and they've got you. I made good money out of town, a thousand bucks a week in Stratford. But that's where I OD'd the first time on cocaine. Excellent cocaine. I bought it off the waitress. The ambulance came and I told them I was epileptic. But they could tell because of my needled arms. The DJ there was a jerk, but he had needles because he was diabetic with lots of clean needles for speed and cocaine.

When I was living on Hamilton Road, there was a guy named Rick who lived around the corner. We were both alcoholic buddies, drank together every day. Some girl, a goof, who liked Rick, came over and stabbed me. I never ratted on her. I have never been a stool pigeon. That's why I'm alive and no one is looking for me. I can go walk down my main street right now.

**Patricia**: You stripped for a period and then Tommy was released from jail.

**Kelly**: He was on a pass, living in a half way house. We were shooting up coke one day and he said, "Kelly, mix up the rest." I mixed it up and gave it all to him but it was enough for three people. I accidentally OD'd him. We were in a federal half way house up in his apartment. Next thing I knew there is a knock at the door. It was staff telling him it was time for a meeting. He went down and he pulled it off. Isn't that amazing?

We were sitting in a hotel room and I had saved up about a thousand dollars. I was reading the Inquirer and I said, "Oh ya, I think I'm pregnant." He said, "I don't think so." Then I kept getting high and I'd puke. I said, "This dope is shit." But everybody else liked it.

**Patricia**: So you told Tommy that you thought you were pregnant. Did you use protection with all these different men?

**Kelly**: What different men?

**Patricia**: Art?

**Kelly**: Ya. I slept with him. But I wasn't a tramp. I had a name for not being a tramp. Tommy tried. He offered me a quarter ounce of speed worth $500 and I told him "No."

**Patricia**: I had the impression that many young women in this kind of scene traded sex for drugs.

**Kelly**: Some do. Some don't. I was with Tommy for years. Art and Tommy were it.

**Patricia**: How were things when you were pregnant with James?

**Kelly**: I was shooting up cocaine and I overdosed when I was in my second month and didn't really know yet. I was young and didn't realize it was a real, live baby. I'd do a hit, that's doing an injection with cocaine when I was eight months pregnant. The baby would roll and kick. We'd just laugh and think it was funny. I didn't realize. These days the Children's Aid step in. My doctors knew, they were supportive, excellent doctors. They knew. I was honest with them. Now they legally would have to take action. Then they didn't.

**Patricia**: What was James' birth like?

**Kelly**: I was kind of nervous. I remember when he was born asking, "Does he have all his legs, arms, toes and that?" Then they took him to observation for forty-four hours. When he was born, Oh My God! That was when I realized he was a human.

**Patricia**: It was like an awakening for you.

**Kelly**: Huge. I fell right in love with him.

**Patricia**: During the birth itself, were you high?

**Kelly**: No. I might have been a little hung over.

**Patricia**: Do you remember feeling any discomfort or pain?

**Kelly**: Oh ya. It hurt like hell. But he was healthy. He was a little shaky when he was born.

**Patricia**: I remember visiting after James was born. You and Tommy were living in a little basement apartment. How were things when you took James home?

**Kelly**: Tommy was in the half way house when I was pregnant with James. He was on parole when we moved into the basement. He quit doing everything. He didn't do anything any more.

**Patricia**: Did you stop at the same time?

**Kelly**: No. I used more.

**Patricia**: So who supplied you with drugs if he was not using drugs?

**Kelly**: I just went out and got it. I'd go out and bring home three or four grams. It was hard because James was awake eighteen hours a day. We would take shifts to look after him. I slowed down for quite awhile.

**Patricia**: So you could not take care of the baby's needs.

**Kelly**: I was a good mom. I was taking him to the Child Reach parent centre.

**Patricia**: Do you know what disrupted this pattern? At some point you moved into Lillian's apartment building.

**Kelly**: We moved in there when I had Danielle. I don't know. Ya, you're right Mom. James was a baby when we moved in there. I had Danielle two years later. I went back to stripping for awhile. When I got pregnant with her I really cut down on everything because I felt so bad when James was born. I learned my lesson. I barely even smoked cigarettes. I don't think I did cocaine at all, after about two months being pregnant. Tommy did excellent. Then he got cancer. When Danielle was a baby everything fell apart. She was two weeks old, it was Christmas and we found out he had testicle cancer. He had to have radiation. Danielle was colicky. I was going to school and working.

**Patricia**: Would you have been using drugs while handling all that?

**Kelly**: Well, ya. I was pretty hung over at school. I used on the weekends. All week I didn't use anything.

**Patricia**: So Monday to Friday you did not use?

**Kelly**: Well, maybe beer but I stayed off the needles. That was really hard and I got my credits; ninety-seven percent in Math and ninety-eight percent in English. I was working full-time. Tommy was sick and it was too much.

**Patricia**: When you say it was too much, does that mean that both of you started using again?

**Kelly**: I don't really remember, Mom. I do remember we moved on to Euclid Street and it was a beautiful three bedroom place. That was nice. I really loved that place. You and Dad gave me a washer and dryer. But I started drinking an awful lot.

**Patricia**: I remember you started fighting with Tommy and eventually kicked him out.

**Kelly**: Ya, I did. I remember I was taking the kids to Child Reach every day. I was taking them for wagon rides all over the place. I was really good to them, then. I stayed out of jail. There was a lady that worked at Proudfoot, a half way house, that lived down the street named Judy. She knew me in jail and she said she remembered me back then. She said I was the best mom. My kids were always clean, happy and smiling. The kids were about three and two years old, if that. Then I kicked Tommy out and things really fell apart. I did great for a while, though. Tommy would take the kids on weekends and I did fine. I was staying clean. Then I started going out and partying. I met Rob. He is from a crime family. I got into the drugs really bad. Then Tommy got back into the drugs from hanging around me and Rob.

**Patricia**: So you met Rob and he moved in with you.

**Kelly**: Ya. He moved in with me and we just started getting high together. I don't know how I kept the kids alive. He was a big time dealer. He got busted for five and half kilograms. He got busted for two Cadillacs, his Jag, my Fiero, about ten thousand dollars of diamonds of mine.

**Patricia**: These were stolen things?

**Kelly**: No. We bought them with dope money. He was extremely violent. He locked me and the kids in the house for six weeks in the summer.

**Patricia**: What other ways was he violent? Did he hit you?

**Kelly**: No. Not me, but if anyone looked at me wrong.

**Patricia**: If anyone looked at you wrong they got punched out?

**Kelly**: Yup. Big time.

**Patricia**: Did he have guns in the house?

**Kelly**: Oh ya! When he went out on business, he would pay his buddies to make sure I stayed in the house.

**Patricia**: When you say that you do not know how you kept the kids alive, what do you mean?

**Kelly**: I remember once James saying that he was starving and I couldn't get my head together enough to make a peanut butter sandwich.

**Patricia**: So you were using drugs heavily.

**Kelly**: Big time. I remember James put on his little pajamas to watch Postman Pat and I was fried. I was as high as a kite from the night before and he would say, "Hi Mom," and sit down quietly in front of the TV. He was scared. He was kicked out of his room. Rob took over his room, moved all his dope stuff in there so James didn't have a room anymore. James wasn't allowed to knock on the door because Rob would flip on him. He was petrified of Rob. Once Rob came in and James and Danielle both freaked out, screaming and hysterical. But he would go to Toys R Us and get four or five hundred dollars of toys.

**Patricia**: So that was his way of showing affection. Was this when some kind of chemical lab was set up in your home?

**Kelly**: It was going all the time. We were cooking twenty-four hours, cooking up rock. We would buy powder and cook it up ourselves. He only trusted me to do it. Most people cook it in a spoon because they only have a little bit. We cooked it in eight ounce baby jars. We would have to break the baby jars to break out the rock, it would be so big. You have to mix it with baking soda and some water. You put it on low. When it goes like a film, a greasy film, you spin it. Then you get it into cold water. If you don't keep spinning it, it will stick to the sides. If you keep spinning it and spinning it, twirling it, it will go into a perfect ball.

**Patricia**: Then you sold the rock?

**Kelly**: Then we had to package up like, fifty-eight packages. We'd fall asleep with the dope, spill it all over. He'd fall asleep cooking and knock over a quarter ounce, like six hundred bucks worth. James knew how to cook a rock from start to finish. One day he had a mixing bowl and a can of coca-cola and he had baking soda. I said, "What are you doing?" He was about three. He said, "I'm making a rock, Mom." I'd catch him scraping crack pipes.

**Patricia**: Did the drugs come from Montreal?

**Kelly**: No, Florida. Our dealer is one of the most wanted men in Canada right now. He got away. I overdosed eight times. Once with Tommy when I was pregnant with James, once before I met him and five times while I lived with Rob. Tommy was really bad into it. He was over every day bugging us. I was down to actually weighing about ninety pounds.

**Patricia**: What do you do with this thing called "a rock?"

**Kelly**: You smoke it in a pipe.

**Patricia**: What happened that things changed again?

**Kelly**: It was getting too nuts. Rob was never coming home. He'd go out for a week and send over dope, milk and diapers. I'd stay awake twenty-four hours a day until the weekend and Tommy came for the kids. Then Rob would want to go to Niagara Falls or Florida. I'd be too burned. I'd sleep. I wasn't having any fun at all. So I kicked him out. I regretted it because I lost my dope, TV and car. But then he got busted two weeks later.

**Patricia**: You moved to Hamilton. You were in a woman's interval home planning to start a new life.

**Kelly**: What happened there, a girl—you know I can take all responsibility for myself now—she was going out and getting crack all the time across the street. She brought me home a toke once.

**Patricia**: What is a toke?

**Kelly**: Crack.

**Patricia**: What is crack?

**Kelly**: Crack. Dope. It's rock cocaine.

**Patricia**: Thank you. So she brought drugs to the women's home.

**Kelly**: Ya, and the next night she wanted to go out and against my better judgement, I really didn't want to, stupidly, I did go. I made my own choice to take a toke. I did one toke. I didn't know my way back. I had to find my own way back. I told the staff what happened. She left me down town. She got kicked out. I was given another chance. But then I came home drunk, I ended up in detox in Hamilton. Tommy had taken the kids for the weekend in London.

**Patricia**: That's right and then the children lived with Tommy and Lillian for a number of years. So, somehow you got yourself back to London. Do you remember with whom you lived?

**Kelly**: No.

**Patricia**: You lived with whomever? I remember you lived with several different guys and a woman.

**Kelly**: Yup. Dee. She got nailed for trafficking. Then I really got into all kinds of shit, in the papers and in a standoff.

**Patricia**: Then you rolled a stolen car, cracked your vertebrae, needed to wear a neck brace and ended up staying with us in Burlington for a couple of nights to convalesce until you went to a bar to watch a hockey game.

**Kelly**: I had a great big bash going upstairs of the bar with air force pilots. They drove me part way to London and then I hitchhiked. I threw the neck brace into the ditch. They wanted me to stay. We had a ball. We had that place rocking.

**Patricia**: You were in the *London Free Press*. You had the swat team involved?

**Kelly**: Oh, ya. They were on roofs and everything. So I used Annette's name. Well, didn't she have a warrant out for her. I was hauled in anyways. I was pissed off. They said, "I see you missed court."

**Patricia**: Who was your favourite judge?

**Kelly**: Definitely Judge L. She's excellent. She's fair, respectful. She nods and smiles in the court room and treats you like a human being. We were getting on a first name basis. I was getting ready to call her "Janie" (laugh). She said, "Hi Kelly." She didn't get disgusted like Judge X. He kicked me out of his court three times.

**Patricia**: She didn't kick you out?

**Kelly**: No. But he did. Laugh, my God. Marilyn and I were in the prisoner's box at the same time and they were saying how a cop bent over and that Marilyn started hooping him in the ass. I didn't know this part of the story so I was just roaring and laughing. She got the giggles and we almost fell out of the box we were laughing so hard. She's the one that went to rehab last month but left. Judge L. said, "Kelly, I'm going to give you another break." My lawyer had asked for six months. The prosecution had asked for nine months. Usually a judge would say seven months. Her! She said, "Three months." She's really human. She would say, "How are you, Kelly? What happened this time?" Plus she smiles, sometimes, if I did something funny.

**Patricia**: So, she has a sense of humour. Who else do you feel appreciation for from your old life?

**Kelly**: Dr. Dorothy Hawswell, who delivered my children. Staff at the medical clinic I used in London. They have been my life line for ten years. Oh, man. I'd come in and there'd be a long waiting line. As soon as I walked through the door they'd bring me right into the office. It's true. Once they told me I'd have to wait a minute and I was gone.

**Patricia**: They really understood and accepted you.

**Kelly**: Big time. They would give me a hug and tell me that they loved me. They sent me to the hospital in an ambulance because they didn't trust that I would go in a cab. They figured I'd go to the beer store instead. If it wasn't for them, I wouldn't have gone to get the stitches out of my head and stuff like that—which I almost didn't do. I said, "Can I wait another day cause I'm a little bit drunk right now?" They said, "Honey, just come on in. Just have a beer waiting for you at home." I always respected them, big time.

**Patricia**: I feel curious about what was really happening around the time I wrote you certain letters. Are you up to a bit more?

*July 5, 1993 Letter* (see pages 40 – 41)

**Patricia**: You landed in the hospital again. What happened?

**Kelly**: A guy I was going out with was just jealous. We were drunk right in a restaurant. He was being rude to a friend I liked. I told him he was being rude. He said, "Well, if you like him so much, go with him." I leaned down to put on my sandal and bonk, right in my back he stabbed me. He pulled his knife right out of the steak. Talk about tactless.

**Patricia**: He ran and the ambulance came. Did you ever report his name?

**Kelly**: Never.

**Patricia**: That is the code of ethics of the . . . ?

**Kelly**: Not being a stool pigeon, being solid. I wouldn't testify against him or anything.

**Patricia**: So, that is the code of ethics in the drug world. Is that the correct word?

**Kelly**: No. It's the street scene.

**Patricia**: So, it is the code of ethics on the street. Thank you.

*November 13, 1993 Letter* (see pages 43 – 44)

**Kelly**: I lived in a party house. Two guys lived there and worked. I never slept with either of them. My buddy, Stan, lived across the hall. It was very small. It was a small place but we had good party times. I was the wildest one. None of them did dope, just drank. That's where I met Jeff. I remember that day. I was there when I made fun of your idea of going to AA. I actually expected you to see the humour of me telling you "Ya, Ma, I go to NA and the PTA. too." Now I understand it wasn't funny to you.

*February 22, 1994 Letter* (see pages 45)

**Patricia**: How did your jaw really get broken?

**Kelly**: Steve broke my jaw. I left it hanging for two weeks, sort of held it together.

**Patricia**: He punched you?

**Kelly**: Ya. I saw stars. He was very violent. He has been in jail for attempted murder. I went out with him when I was younger. I stayed with him a couple nights before and partied. We got drunk. The next day I had arranged to go see the kids. So, I had to leave his house unlocked. I left my friend Bonnie there to watch his house and two pounds of pot went missing. Guess who he thought took it. I've done a lot of dirty things in my life but I was not known as a thief to my friends. He came up and he was already pissed off because someone had ripped him off for some money. He just gave me a slap across the jaw.

**Patricia**: A slap?

**Kelly**: Ya. Open handed and then a broken jaw in two places. He's wicked. Then I held my jaw back together and my friend went to get some ice and did some tokes. About a week or so later the jaw got abscessed and that really hurt. So I had surgery and they wired it up. I only stayed three days. We had a big party in my hospital room and I ended up leaving. Lloyd brought up a forty ouncer (vodka) and a ball of dope. I had a bad hangover and I thought I was going to be sick so I snipped the wires. I didn't want to puke to death.

**Patricia**: When you drank alcohol you drank vodka. You also drank beer.

**Kelly**: Vodka is my favourite. I drank anything. But I was not a rubbing alcohol girl. Let's clarify. I was not a scrubbing girl like the ones that drink rubbing alcohol.

**Patricia**: So you were never so desperate that you would drink rubbing alcohol?

**Kelly**: No. So that's what happened with my jaw. I wound up clipping the wires, got busted and had to go to jail with the braces on and the wires clipped.

**Patricia**: So he was never charged?

**Kelly**: Hell, no. I still partied with him up 'till last summer. I always told him, "You know, that's one thing I never did. I never took that weed and you owe me an apology." I always told him that. Straight up.

**Patricia**: Did he ever give you an apology?

**Kelly**: He never did. He heard I was selling. I said to him, "Ya, you tell me to who?" I said, "Don't you tell me that Steve. That's bullshit." I've always wanted an apology for that. To this day I still feel cheated. It still bothers me to this day.

**Patricia**: It's hard when you are accused of something you did not do.

*April 18, 1994 Letter* (see pages 48)

**Patricia**: You were in jail because you were in some kind of stand off with the police.

**Kelly**: I held off the London Police Force and the Swat team, me and three other people. I got charged for living off the proceeds of trafficking a narcotic, unlawful, unsafe storage of a firearm and something else.

**Patricia**: Was this one of those situations where you were at the wrong place at the wrong time?

**Kelly**: No. I went over to give him a toke of my dope. I was there and I did up a friend's coat. Mike, a friend of mine, was going out with shotgun shells and he couldn't fit his jacket over it.

**Patricia**: Was this a dealer's place and he had a stockpile of drugs? You were going over to share even when he had more than you?

**Kelly**: So? That doesn't matter.

**Patricia**: I want to understand. Did you owe him something? Or just friends to hang out with?

**Kelly**: It's Steve. The one that broke my jaw. What happened, was Mike was leaving, and I did up his coat over the shotgun shells because it didn't fit. Then I said, "Mike, there's a coper." He said, "Oh, fuck him." Then two more cops came around the corner saying "Get on your knees, face down." Then Steve yelled down the stairs, "Is that the cops?" I said, "Ya" and he said, "Well, shut the door." So I shut the door and went upstairs.

    We could see the cops pointing their guns and shit. The SWAT team came. Then they phoned. Julian Fantino, the chief of police of London, phoned and said, "Morgan, come out with your hands up." I said, "Fuck you." We just turned up the tunes, drank and flushed about ten zillion pills down the toilet. I hooped an ounce, twenty-eight grams of crack, I took into jail that night. We just cleaned the house quick—dropped the guns down some holes in the wall.

**Patricia**: So you were eventually taken away by the police.

**Kelly**: Ya. But I had an ounce of dope I took out. If you hoop it, it hurts, right?

**Patricia**: Wait. What's "hooping it" mean?

**Kelly**: Putting it in your crotch. Twenty-eight grams of it. So, I was sore. At the police station it was hurtin' so I took it out and put it in the front of my jeans. Well, didn't they call me for fingerprints? I got up and I had a big lump. Oh! I swear one cop looked right at it but said nothing.

**Patricia**: You took the drug into jail with you.

**Kelly**: Oh ya. I had the whole range high for three days. Girls took showers and came back buck naked, all too stoned forgetting they were wet and barenaked sitting down at the picnic table.

**Patricia**: You created a party in the Elgin Middlesex Detention Centre.

**Kelly**: Oh ya. People have never forgotten that one. But I wasn't smart. My partner, Janice, she was in there with me, through the whole stand off. I gave her part of the dope. She went and made like eight hundred bucks. I didn't even make a pack of smokes. She was collecting bills after she got out. You believe that? She got everybody's canteen. She made a killing. We had a blast. The girls were sending their food trays back full. That's like a dead give away. I said, "This range is cut off. Flush your meal down the toilet and Lorraine quit jonesing on the floor. Get up."

**Patricia**: She was what, on the floor?

**Kelly**: When your crack is all gone or even when you have some left you Jones, you look for more. I don't want to explain it but I had fifteen jonesers on my hands. They were fighting.

**Patricia**: It is like an altered consciousness, or freaking out?

**Kelly**: Oh ya. That's why I was in jail. I was prepared to take two charges—the weapons or the dope, since I got the dope. See, the cops didn't find any drugs at all. What they did was, they dropped a crumb outside the window and said that one of the girls threw it out the window. It didn't stick anyways.

**Patricia**: I am not sure I am following. They threw a "crumb" out the window?

**Kelly**: When they can't find dope and they just held up the entire London Police force for hours and the SWAT team, they have to say something and they can't charge you with nothing. So, they throw down a little piece of dope and charge everybody for trafficking. They put it there, their own damn self, all the time. I don't know how they explain all that, but it looks good in the paper—these five charged for traffickers. But I had the last laugh. I got high all weekend. Man, primo dope and if that's not good enough, I got thrown into the hole and by the date my dope was all gone, I was released. I had to go home and sleep (laugh).

**Patricia**: You were released because?

**Kelly**: Mike took all the charges. All the rest of us got out. They said, "Morgan, you are out of here."

**Patricia**: Is that when you phoned us, asking for $500 bail?

**Kelly**: Ya. I'm glad you didn't send it. That would have screwed everything up. If I sat around smoking an ounce of Steve's dope, I would have owed him twenty-eight hundred dollars. But he was happy because I hid it.

*June 8, 1994 Letter* (see page 51)

**Patricia**: In April you asked us for bail. We said, "No" and did not have contact with you until September. By June I was feeling frantic not hearing from you. Were you feeling angry with us?

**Kelly**: Yes I was angry. To tell the truth, I felt abandoned for the first time from you. It was tough on me. I thought I had finally lost you.

**Patricia**: You believed that I had given up on you, although we said saying "no" to bail had nothing to do with loving you.

**Kelly**: Ya. I couldn't believe it. So I felt depressed. I just gave up. I thought you had really cut me loose.

**Patricia**: Though we said, we had not.

**Kelly**: Right. I don't remember that part.

**Patricia**: In the end you say that saying "no" was smart for us to do.

**Kelly**: Right.

*September 6, 1994 Letter* (see pages 52 – 53)

**Patricia**: I finally found you at Vanier's Institute for Women in Brampton. What was that like?

**Kelly**: I loved it. I had a ball. I was in with my street partner. We were selling dope in there. She had a boyfriend come visit her every week and it was open visit there. They'd kiss and he'd pass her a couple grams of dope. We were the only ones on our range—fried, really fried. We had girls offering us their shoes for a toke.

I was supposed to peel potatoes for Ann, the cook, and I'd be too burned out from smoking dope all night. I'd fall asleep in the kitchen. So I got fired from the kitchen and sent to the laundry. I got fired out of the laundry. I wound up on house cleaning. My roommate and I were the mouthiest. She was like four foot nothing. She'd say, "Oh shut up, you fuckin' goof," to everybody in the next cell. We would be so high we'd be laughing and carrying on. The girls would say, "Will you fuckers shut up and sleep?" Lorraine would say, "Fuck you. My roommate's going to punch you out in the morning." But they would still mess around.

We wound up having a good time. But I was kicked out of there and sent back to triple maximum security. We were all ready to run. You can get out of there. You just have to hop a couple of fences. We had on jail shoes. They're blue shoes with white toes. I said, "Come on, let's split." She said, "Right on, we're out of here." She goes and crayons all her shoes so nobody knows they're jail shoes. You get jeans there so you look pretty normal. Then she remembered we only had three weeks left so we decided we'd stay. So, I had a lot of fun there. I really liked it there. I was in with all the girls from London. As soon as I walked in the door, boom, they gave me whole packs of cigarettes and chocolate bars, chips and pop. So I felt like . . .

**Patricia**: At home and appreciated.

**Kelly**: Ya, missed, loved. Catch up on the gossip. They knew I was good for a couple poor efforts a day. If you put your feet up on a couch, that's a poor effort. If you swear or don't do your chore that's a poor effort. If you get three poor efforts then you get an extra day. I was there a week and I had nineteen poor efforts (laugh). So, I put in to be sent back to London or I would never get out of there. They'd say, "Morgan, get your feet down." I'd say, "Oh, Fuck!" Then I'd get another poor effort right there. They trick you like that (laugh). They had a blast with that. I had the girls just killin' themselves laughin'. I had a lot of fun there.

Finally, they decided that all I could do was clean windows by myself—not near anyone else working. The windows would be spotless. They gave us hallways with all windows. They'd put each of us at a window. Peaceful. Dead quiet. No banging. Nothing going on. I was fine. But it was too damn late with those nineteen poor efforts.

**Patricia**: Were you still using drugs, though?

**Kelly**: Oh, ya. Man, we had Valium, rock and we never got caught.

**Patricia**: What were you doing in jail again?

**Kelly**: I don't know. Assault, probably. Possession. Whatever. I got out of my handcuffs on the way to the jail. We were handcuffed behind our backs and shackled. I took my cuffs off and helped Lorraine take her's off. We were going down the 401 and they pulled over at MacDonald's. I said, "Oh good, Lorraine. It looks like we get a hamburger." They said, "Morgan, get up here," and they tugged the cuffs really tight. They told the lady at Vanier's, "We've got one for you."

I knew the girls from Kitchener. It was a big camp. We stole food. We had our pockets full of date squares. Man, we ate good. You can suntan. Posters all over our walls, just like home. Mail call! Lorraine and me, one day we got sixteen mails. From everybody, girls from the jails, girls I knew in London and people from the street. That was really cool. I felt loved. We'd make a big show of it at breakfast. We'd drop a couple by accident. "Oh, guess who else wrote Lorraine?" (laugh) We loved it. I'd put my feet up on the table and get another poor effort.

*September 26, 1994 Letter* (see pages 56)

**Kelly**: They said, "We can't handle you no more," and they put me in the hole for thirty days.

**Patricia**: You are saying that when you arrived back in London they put you in the hole. Why?

**Kelly**: When I went on the range all the girls started asking, "How's it going?" I sauced the guard and threatened to take her head off.

**Patricia**: That is why you were sent back to London?

**Kelly**: Ya. They didn't even warn me. They said nothing. Didn't even give me another poor effort. They said, "Your ride is here. Get going." The guard, Janet, let me smoke in the van on the way back. She's all right. But there are some cops that aren't decent. The most dirty guy I've ever met framed me. He pulled over the car, threw dope at my feet and said, "Oh, I found your dope." He looked me dead in the eye, laughed at me, hauled me into the station and charged me. There's a lot of dirtiness out there.

*October 8, 1994 Letter* (see pages 70 – 71)

**Kelly**: At that time I went to Quinton Warner House, a drug treatment program in London. Why did I go there? I don't know. I went there for about a month. I liked it but I wasn't ready for it. I was the only lady. There was twenty-eight men and me. All the men lived there. I lived at Rothhome and I had to walk to get there everyday. Meanwhile, Maggie lived across the street and partied.

I used G.H. for a lawyer. I am up in front of a judge under a fake name and he says, "Kelly, you've gotta tell the judge your real name." I said, "Well. You are fired!" Tommy ripped that lawyer off for a thousand bucks.

**Patricia**: So, you got even. Girls would find you in the washroom to buy drugs in the court house.

**Kelly**: Hell, yes.

**Patricia**: While you were being heard on charges. You would be as high as a kite?

**Kelly**: I was very drunk in front of Judge C. once. I had been out partying. I hardly made it to court. It was one of the few times I actually showed up on my own free will. I was so drunk. I went to lean on my lawyer's table, just caught the corner and down I went. I was only asked to come sober next time.

Mr. B. is my man. He's a good lawyer. He's straight up. He's solid. Well, he works your case, as a lawyer should. He's a good man, too. He'd come out and visit me at the jail. He treated me with respect and I have the utmost respect for him.

I've been thinking why I never had any fear is because up until this year, I couldn't put together action and consequence. I could not tie them in. My whole life has been each individual minute at a time in the present.

**Patricia**: And if the present was crappy, get out of it?

**Kelly**: Change it, fast! I never, ever saw any connection, and this is God's truth, between action and consequence. So I'd be sitting in a courtroom up on a bunch of charges and not thinking, until I'd say to my lawyer, "You fuckin' goof, you're fired," and see who I could make laugh in the courtroom. That was in this second. What I'm there for, that's already happened. I didn't see how my actions would eventually get me another fifteen days. Then I'd be so mad when I'd get those extra days. I honestly couldn't tie together my actions and the consequences. I still have trouble with it.

Now I know. Take doing laundry, for example. If I had no clean clothes I used to think, "I better go steal some clothes." Now, I do my laundry. I'm starting to see how my actions can produce an acceptable, even positive result.

**Patricia**: Is time a problem partly because you live so much in the present?

**Kelly**: Ya. I can't judge if five minutes or an hour has gone by.

**Patricia**: That is common. When it's pleasurable an hour feels like five minutes.

**Kelly**: No. I really can't tell. Same with autistic people. They have no sense of time.

**Patricia**: Speaking of time, thank you so much for taking the time to tell me some of your story.

**Kelly**: You're welcome, Mom. I love you.

# 6
# ...update

NINE YEARS HAVE PASSED SINCE KELLY SAID "YES MOM," back on July 18, 1995 at the Elgin-Middlesex Detention Centre in London, Ontario. The rush of exhilaration I felt in hearing that answer is still with me. From that moment, our relationship matured. After dropping the children off at Lillian's, I drove back to Toronto, returned my friend's car and took a bus to my mother's home in Fenelon Falls. I spent a week there before Kelly's release but felt I needed to stay longer. Changing the date of my return flight was the first thing to which I attended. I made an extensive, over-the-telephone search for a suitable treatment centre or program in both the provinces of Ontario and Alberta. Les requested the services of an employee assistance counsellor from his place of employment and she kindly explored the possibilities in Alberta. Many of the organizations I contacted requested that Kelly send a letter of application, which would be followed by a phone call and then a screening interview. Impossible! I was to return to Calgary. Kelly had no fixed address. One intake worker told me, "Now, Mom, it sounds like you are doing all the work. It is time for you to realize that your daughter is a grown woman. If she is ready to get well, she will phone us and make the arrangements. Promise me you will let go of the strings and let her take care of herself." Condescending or what?

Other voices, however, were supportive and encouraging. One telephone receptionist told me, "I used to be a drunk. Now I am OK and have a job I love at this treatment centre." I asked if there had been someone there for her throughout her troubled period. Her answer was, "My mother." Feeling connected and energized I blurted out, "Well, I am the mother!"

Of all the treatment centres I called: Hope Place, Breton House, Harmony House, Brock Cottage, Homewood, Stonehenge, Thames Valley, Renaissance, Donwood, Bellwood, Brant House, Women's Own Detox, it was only the last, House of Sophrosyne, that provided immediate encouragement and support to me, would soon have a bed available, and agreed to conduct a screening interview with Kelly over the phone.

Kelly, Jamie, Mary, Danielle and Patricia in Fenelon Falls in 1995.

A week later I picked Kelly up at the Elgin-Middlesex Detention Centre. She was wearing a short skirt, a white T-shirt and a pair of running shoes. She strutted out a back door waving goodbye to her inmate friends, had a big grin, walked toward me with outstretched arms and said, "Hi Mom." I asked about other clothes and belongings. She told me that her stuff was at the home of a drug dealer. "So? We will just go up to that apartment and get your things," I said. "No way," she responded. Kelly explained to me that if she went in with her straight mother and if she went in alone her chances of her coming out again were slim. "I'm still addicted, Mom." So we agreed to start fresh — clothes, undies, toiletries, an alarm clock, a hair dryer and a carry case for all of it.

While finding a bank and attending to our shopping in downtown London, Kelly, with me, her mother, at her side, was approached three times by drug dealers. They made a signal with their hand to their ear and made eye contact. She would tell me, "See this guy coming up the street. Watch, he's a dealer and he'll check out whether I'm in the market or not."

It was with relief that I arrived in Fenelon Falls with Kelly. For more than two weeks my mother and I *babysat an addict*. Kelly was restless most days and we had moments of tension just holding on to the idea of her going into treatment. For the first time in my life I agreed to go to Bingo. Bingo is one of the social highlights of Fenelon Falls and Kelly enjoyed the activity. I gather some feel quite excited playing the game. The smoky environment was not my idea of mother-daughter bonding but I was pleased she seemed to enjoy my company. We also arranged to have James and Danielle come for a four-day visit. It meant more driving for me but that seemed a minor inconvenience compared with the potential pay off.

We discovered that Kelly had abscessed teeth that required two separate trips to Oshawa to see a dental surgeon. Two teeth were removed. When she came out of the surgery woozy from the anesthesia she rested on a couch with her head on my lap. I felt so tender. I quietly sang to her, *"You are my sunshine, my only sunshine. You make me happy when skies are grey. You'll never know dear, how much I love you. Please don't take my sunshine away."* Meanwhile, if she felt any energy, she insisted that we get up and leave. "I don't stay in places like this. They fix me and then I go." However, the dental assistants were insisting that she settle down and rest. I thought, "Seldom does this Kelly of ours rest."

My mom was a super presence for both Kelly and me. She cooked and fussed over us just the right amount. At night, after Kelly had gone to bed, she would give me some useful observations or offer an idea about how we might better calm Kelly in some of her frustrated moments. Kelly responded quickly and eagerly to her grandmother's requests. Because of her grandma, she also attempted to dampen her street-trained vocabulary. What a fine senior lady my mom is. Both Kelly and I are quite bonded and in love with her.

On August 13, Kelly and I drove to the House of Sophrosyne, a women's treatment centre in Windsor, Ontario. We walked up to the front door and Kelly said, "I've changed my mind. I'm not doing this." I felt my body energy drain, my knees weaken, my thinking blur and could hardly breathe. Then she said she was just kidding. "Some joke," I thought. I felt blessed when we were gently and kindly received on the other side of the door. A couple of days later, I returned to Calgary and the rest of my family.

Kelly stayed for three months and made frequent, often daily, phone calls to me in Calgary. I felt thrilled to be acknowledged as her support person. It was like a big door had opened bringing light and clarity. She was committed to the healing process and liked her counsellors. Weekly I was impressed with how caringly, yet firmly, the staff worked and helped mend our Kelly. My mother, Les, and I started to refer to Kelly's new openness and appreciation of help as "a miracle."

This miracle provided us with a new beginning. In the previous three or four years, I had heard about Attention Deficit Disorder (ADD) and had wondered if Kelly fit the diagnosis. Now, for the first time, she was in an emotionally receptive state to explore the possibility of an assessment. I remember Kelly asking me over the phone, "Mom, do you think I have something like that? Wouldn't that be something to find out that I'm not really just plain bad?" Yet a part of her wondered what an ADD diagnosis would mean. With the help of Dr. Teeya Scholten, an ADD specialist and friend, I forwarded a questionnaire to Kelly and her treatment counsellor. Soon after, an appointment was made with a psychiatrist, who told her that she has an extreme case of ADHD. It was amazing for Kelly and me to go through the list of indicators. Both of us had memory flashbacks of old incidents that felt crazy making at the time. We thought, "Oh, no wonder." The diagnosis explained so much. The "H" refers to the hyperactive form of Attention Deficit.

When we were raising Kelly, she was viewed by professionals as a child with some nasty label such as Conduct Disorder or Sociopath, or her behaviour was viewed as totally the result of parent mishandling by Les and me. Hyperactivity was talked about twenty years ago but little was known about effective management. Back then it was also believed that "children will outgrow it." Well, I have learned that 80% of people do not. Kelly is one of them.

In 1986 an official definition of ADD-RT, the RT referring to Residual Type, which applies to adults, came from an article by Dr. David Woods. It stated that an adult must have exhibited ADD symptoms as a child. After that, the person must have attention span deficiency, motor abnormalities and at least two of the following symptoms: poor impulse control, low stress tolerance with emotional over-reaction to stress, poor organization with poor task completion, and extreme mood swings in response to events in the external environment, or short, excessive temper. Feelings of anger, confusion, frustration, and low self-esteem are natural consequences of such a life. Finally! Many of Kelly's lifelong behaviours made sense and were given a context of meaning that was previously missing.

Kelly is among many teens and adults with ADD who have found escape in alcohol and street drugs. Indeed, she spent a large part of the last eleven years in jail because of self-medicating with alcohol and cocaine. Ritalin on the streets, Kelly tells me, is the poor person's speed. Now I understand that she was unconsciously trying to feel *normal*.

Realizing what ADD is provided relief for Kelly, me, and the many people who have struggled with her unpredictable behaviour. However, I do not want to imply that Kelly does not have issues from a confusing and disruptive childhood. Research suggests that a high percentage of people with ADD had rocky life beginnings. But what a comfort to discover that all those chores not done, items lost, poor school performances, forgotten messages, impulsive and bizarre behaviours, and numerous lies to cover up these activities were because of being challenged with ADD. The chaotic and impulsive behaviours were not from some label of personality disorder or triggered by mother regression neurosis. The diagnosis was healing to both Kelly and me. ADD does not explain all of Kelly's involvement with substance abuse. Yet it provided a major piece to a fragmented puzzle for her. Piece by piece, she began to create a picture of who she is and what she wants for herself and her children.

When I presented the idea of this book to her, she said, "Sounds cool, Mom. I trust you." This was a different person who spoke with confidence and trusted my integrity. I started to recognize that I was different after the journey I had been on with her. To have participated with Kelly when she began to move into the *other* world, into *our* world where I, her Dad, and family function, is thrilling for me.

She had more to learn and tragedies from which to heal. Like a baby beginning to take steps, Kelly was at the beginning of learning many things. She had numerous educational, emotional and social developmental lags challenging her. *Incredibly*, she did not seem to have suffered much brain damage. However, she missed a tremendous amount of *normal* living.

Life skills were, initially, an unknown to her. She needed to learn that the price tag on an item was not the total cost; GST and Ontario provincial tax are added. The telephone is invaluable. I invited her questions: "How do I put money in the bank? What am I supposed to do with the little book they gave me at the bank? What's this thing about registering the kid's for school? How do I find out which school they are supposed to go to? What do I say when I phone the school? What do I say to James' teacher about his problem? How can I say 'no' to the kids when I feel so guilty? How do you ask for a favour? Is it rude to say 'no' if someone asks you to do a favour? Why should I learn to cook? What's wrong with take-out? Should I have thrown out all the food from the freezer when I accidentally let things thaw? When you clean the house each week do you have to wash all the walls? What's protein? Can I lose weight by just eating salad? How do I take back my sweater to the store without saying 'Give me my money or else I'll punch you out!?'"

Finding and utilizing reliable and ethical professionals was a challenge. To my distress Kelly became involved with a psychiatrist who liberally prescribed medication without monitoring. Learning some basic life skills, balancing the use of Ritalin, managing feeling out-of-control and angry, developing and maintaining healthy friendships, regularly attending support meetings, maintaining her commitment to sobriety, and feeling satisfied with a simplified lifestyle were all personal challenges for her.

Kelly arranged for the children to be returned to her care. She created a comfortable home for them and regularly attended support meetings and counselling sessions. In the fall of 1997 she returned to school to complete her secondary education. One of her first papers and class presentations described the symptoms and consequences of having ADHD. We spent hours of telephone time working on

Mary, Patricia, kelly, Jamie and Danielle. A fun summer visit to Fenelon Falls in 1998.

homework assignments. I had longed for that when she was younger. As we talked about linking one paragraph's theme to the next I felt a little giggle of delight in my belly. The excitement Kelly has for learning is heartwarming. Her creativity and humour added fun to our tutoring times. Sometimes she requested her Dad's help on more technical matters making her educational goal even more family-oriented.

When Kelly returned to school her marks were in the nineties, even earning a listing on the University of Windsor president's roll. She began to let her smarts show, began to learn *her* way and asked for a quiet room to write her exams without distractions. Her busy life included psychology and social work classes, parenting, a part-time job and support meetings. She continued her affiliation with Sophrosyne through an alumnae group where she had the opportunity to encourage other young women entering the recovery process. Her struggles and weaknesses increasingly became her gifts and strengths. She was working her buns off to create a different and healthier life for herself and her children.

As with most life roads, not all went smoothly. Physically Kelly struggles with liver damage and other complications from her alcohol and cocaine consumption. Bouts of depression, relapses and spontaneous, and subsequently embarrassing, anger outbursts have occurred; back to the *old and easy ways* have erupted. Most often she called from Ontario to say, "I have something to tell you." She has described, wondered, and asked for the encouragement.

We caught up in bringing her genuinely into the family. James, Danielle and she have spent summer and Christmas holidays with us. She became better connected to her Grandma Mary. In the fall of 1999 they all participated in a beautiful wedding ceremony when Ben married his love light, Chandra. The telephone is a marvellous instrument for relationship maintenance. We have used it to chat, laugh, work on homework, discuss a healthy diet and, sometimes, disagree. Just the other day she said, "The phone was great at the beginning, Mom, but I really want you to come and have a visit. Boy, I miss you."

As often as possible I have traveled from Calgary to Windsor to be in Kelly's home, to participate, to assist with organizational challenges and to be the best mother and grandmother I know how. Our times together have been stimulating and fun. Kelly and I have had many thoughtful discussions about social issues, feminism, personal development and even Oprah. For nearly seven years we danced through many challenges together. I felt rewarded that we were finally bonded as daughter and mother. But what is ever final?

Jamie, Danielle and Kelly at Ben and Chandra's wedding in 1999.

Jamie, Patricia, Les, Danielle, Eric and Kelly in Windsor, December 2003.

In the spring of 2002 Kelly was in her third year of university and my worst fear happened. Kelly showed signs of a deep relapse and by the summer of 2003 had clearly reentered the drug world with many severe consequences. For nearly a year she was lost to all of us who cared, again. Neither she nor I have had the time or opportunity to thoroughly examine this time period.

What I know for sure is this: addictions linger, waiting for moments of weakness. Family and loved ones are thrown into loss and pain. I also know that the longing for health and a bright future can be reclaimed even when the flame of hope is faint.

In January 2003 Kelly entered a three month recovery program in Waterloo, Ontario called Alcontrol. In June she gave birth to dear Eric Mathew and I went to be with her for a period upon his arrival. She talks with more conviction than ever about making her tomorrow a new and healthy beginning for herself and her three children. Recovery meetings are regularly attended. Kelly and I are back in each other's emotional arms with additional mistakes, apologies and forgiveness in our past. Our future has renewed solutions, wonder and possibilities. While this book was written with the intent to share my lessons learned, Kelly continues to be my main teacher.

# Steps in Time

Each beginning brings a new end, and each end, a new beginning.

**Kelly from birth to five years of age:**

1968    Kelly Ann Evoy is born. She is sent back and forth from her mother to foster care until she is finally placed in a foster home.

1971    Kelly is adopted and subsequently sent back to the Etobicoke Children's Aid after nine months.

1973    We meet Kelly in July and on Boxing Day she moves in with us. Ben is just over two years old.

**Kelly from 6 to 10 years of age:**

1974    Soon after adopting Kelly, Les and family are transferred to Sarnia.

1975    Patricia is triggered into feeling out-of-control anger and physically abuses Kelly. She leaves employment and enters group and individual therapy. Kelly and the whole family become involved with the Sarnia-Lambton Centre for Children and Youth.

1976    The family follows Les on a training transfer to England. Patricia is pregnant, depressed and emotionally unstable there.

1977    Back in Canada, at public school, Kelly and her teachers are feeling challenged. Katie is born. With a newborn baby more stress is experienced in the family. Kelly lives, Monday to Friday, at a treatment home for children.

**Kelly from 10 to 15 years of age:**

1978    Kelly returns to public school.

1979    Kelly loves gymnastics.

1982    Problems escalate at public school. At age thirteen, unknown to Patricia and Les, Kelly begins using pot. Kelly is suspended from two high schools and an alternative program.

1983   Kelly attends the Canadian Outward Bound Wilderness School for 3 weeks. By September incidents with peers and police increase.

1984   Kelly is suspended from the alternative program and is assigned an hour of one-on-one teaching daily. When this fails she is required by the school board to work for six months or pass a summer school course before re-entering the educational system. That summer, Kelly leaves home and lives at various locations, including a motorcycle gang's club house. She becomes an active participant in the drug scene but visits home for Christmas.

**Kelly from 16 to 27 years of age:**

1985   Kelly lives briefly at a home for pregnant teenagers. After an operation for hyperbole pregnancy, she resides for less than three weeks at a home for teenage girls. After Kelly is arrested, Patricia has her first visit to a jail. Kelly is transferred to a detention centre and is there for Christmas.

1986   After another term served in jail, Kelly hitchhikes across Canada and back again with friend Annette.

1987   Les, Patricia, Ben and Katie move to Calgary, Alberta.

1988   Kelly and Tommy, her boyfriend, are active in drug dealing.

1989   Seven months pregnant Kelly hitchhikes from Windsor, Ontario to Calgary, Alberta to have a visit with her family. In March, James Eric is born.

1990   Danielle Ann is born.

1992   Les, Patricia and Katie move to Burlington, Ontario. James and Danielle are primarily in the care of their paternal grandmother.

1993   Kelly becomes *a person with no fixed address* and the children move into the full care of their grandmother. Patricia begins to photocopy her letters to Kelly. After a series of injuries, hospital admissions and jail sentences Kelly clearly states to Patricia that she is addicted to alcohol and cocaine. Patricia, Les and Katie move back to Calgary, Alberta.

1994   Kelly writes a letter from jail that describes feelings and beliefs previously unshared. It also indicates that Kelly feels loved by Patricia. Kelly from age 27 to 35 years of age:

1995 Kelly serves a couple more jail sentences with brief periods of freedom between. In May, after release from jail, Kelly is hospitalized with broken cheekbones and other injuries. Patricia transforms her love from *hoping Kelly will change into loving her as she is.* In July, Patricia visits Kelly in jail where she agrees to treatment upon release. Kelly goes into residence at House of Sophrosyne, Windsor, Ontario for three months and decides to settle in that city.

1996   Kelly participates in a number of recovery and agency programs. She reclaims care and responsibility of James and Danielle and moves them to Windsor.

1998   Kelly completes Grade 12.

1999   Kelly begins studies at the University of Windsor.

2000   Kelly becomes a full-time university student, works part-time, attends alumnae meetings and stays actively involved in her children's lives.

2002   A disappointing and deep relapse steals Kelly away from those who love her.

2003   Kelly commits to three months of treatment at Alcontrol, Waterloo, Ontario. She is back on track when Eric Mathew is born in June.

2004   Kelly remains stable while raising her three children.

# 7
# ...Kelly's hints

## Hints for family and friends...

THERE ARE DOZENS OF REASONS ADDICTS START USING DRUGS. Everybody has their own story. It could be they have no one to talk to. There's an acceptance among the drug crowd that not everyone has in their family or community. The lifestyle had the illusion of working for me. Definitely it was full of risks and excitement. Most addicts, though, get hooked because they all like that good feeling. I also think a lot of drug addicts have Attention Deficit Disorder and end up self-medicating.

Mom's letters meant a lot to me. The mere fact that she didn't give up on me and continued to write had an impact on me. I eventually felt reconnected to her and my family. After a lot of accepting on her part, I learned to be more honest with her. The phone calls became easier. The most helpful thing in Mom's letters was that she gave me encouragement over small, healthy things I told her that I had done. A lot of people end up lying to their family just to get a crumb of encouragement. Then the parents get hooked on hope and start building dreams of them kicking their habit. Say "Congratulations" and leave it at that.

Hearing the family news was important to me. I received the message that my family was healthy enough to get on with life. They weren't so worried or torn up about my life that they couldn't function. It comforted me to know that they could stay steady. Mom wrote about Ben doing this and Katie doing that.

What was very helpful was my Mom saying "I love you" a lot. Everyone needs someone to really love them. Another important thing Mom did was she mentioned rehab now and then. I didn't know it at the time but she was planting a seed in my head. It wasn't pushed, or I would have shut her out. She made it clear that the opportunity for rehab was there for me. She and Dad said they would help arrange the treatment and support me financially. That offer of help was clear to me for quite awhile before I agreed.

It was helpful that I could simply tell my Mom what was really going on with me. It took a long time until I was ready to do that. She really earned my trust over a long time. No matter what she was thinking in her head about what I told her, most often she was able to say "I hear you" and not react.

Although I always knew that Mom's love was behind it, sometimes she said things that were not helpful. She would ask, "What are you doing with yourself?" and "What's new in your life?" That was horrible for me because it pointed out to me just how much I wasn't doing with my life. I already knew I was a drug addict, bottom low, living homeless, hooked on needles, trying to find time when I was straight enough (maybe every three or four months) to call her. I'd be proud that I found my family's phone number. Managing to do that, I saw myself as a real family oriented person. I felt proud that I had a family that still loved me, as most addicts don't have that and I was proud of myself for actually phoning. Then she'd ask that question, "What's new with you?" Was I going to say, "I owe the drug dealer fifty bucks, the police are looking for me and I could really use a hot meal?" No. I couldn't say that to my Mother. I'd always say, "Not much. What's new with you?"

I also felt hurt when Mom brought up my past screw ups. I would feel really guilty and go out and get even more high as a direct result. I encourage you to avoid bringing up times your addict disappointed you. An addict is just too messed up to be able to think of how to make amends. What are we supposed to do? We're addicted. That means we're not living responsibly and can't right now.

In some ways, having my parents far away made things easier for me when I was addicted. It wasn't as easy for me to really screw up the relationship. A lot of addicted people go to their parents' homes and rip them off.

Before you put up bail for an addict give it a lot of consideration. Always be very careful about trusting them with anything valuable. However, I recommend to loved ones that they put up bail for their addict, at least once, if they have no reason to believe they won't get their money back. There are different circumstances. Some addicts need to be treated with gentleness and kindness. Others would take caring support as weakness and need a hard line. Every addict is different. Handle your money with caution. I've known parents who have lost their home after putting up bail for their son.

When I came back to consciousness, I noticed that I had a lot of skills from parenting to coping that I learned from my parents. For eleven years, I put little into action that I learned from my family. I sure am now, though. Things I didn't notice when I was growing up did make a difference. I learned things that other people aren't lucky enough to know. Parents need to know that what they model and teach their kids does make a difference. I've seen it in both positive and negative ways.

It was good for me to tell Mom the truth so she could see how much help I needed. I've heard about a lot of parents who freaked or held what they heard against their addict when they were told the truth. Too many don't accept. It was helpful that Mom and Dad got themselves really healthy. Because they could live their own lives, they didn't get all bent out of shape when I told them I was in jail, had broken the law and all that. They didn't blame me or make me out as a bad person so I didn't have to distance myself.

There are some really ignorant parents out there. I mean "ignorant" as uninformed. I've known parents who believed they could control their addict. It is as if they believe they have the power to fix their kid. They will talk about being successful in cleaning up their addict's life, if only they could just figure out the one right thing to do. What a set-up for disappointment. It's like a fantasy they create.

One parent I know used to pay for her daughter's apartment and buy her furniture. The daughter, because she was still using of course, lost the apartment and furniture only to have her mother replace it again and again. I did appreciate that this mother met her daughter every Sunday for coffee. Now this was a healthy move as it kept a line of communication open. If the daughter didn't arrive for those meetings, she lost financial support.

It is important that your addict feels comfortable contacting you at any time. There is a lot of death out there. Hopefully your addict feels safe to contact you and say, "Hi. I am alive." Have, at least, the phone number of two stable people in your addict's life — someone your addict will trust enough to contact now and then — that you can call. When Mom said, "I love you. Please call again," that was valuable. It is important that the parent makes it clear that the phone call was appreciated. Many addicts feel alone, and often are alone. Some die without their parents finding out for a long time. I think Mom was smart to be prepared for my death. I was very close to death many times. The way I was using, I probably had a high chance of dying. It is just by the grace of God that I am not dead.

There's a whole spectrum of parental responses to the issue of addiction in their children, from parents like mine all the way to those who do needles with their kids. One mother had her daughter selling hash oil for her in grade eight. She had to take six vials with her every day to school. I heard her mother died of an overdose. She was a needle addict. It is imperative that parents set a good example. Parents don't realize what an influence they have over their children. A lot of the hugging and reassuring that I give to my children now, I learned from Mom. People say, "Where did she learn that?" Well, I learned it as a kid.

It is rare that an addict intentionally or unintentionally robs her parents or grandparents. We are "borrowing" the money and "intend" to repay it. That is the way most addicts think. "I will borrow from my husband's wallet or pawn my Mom's ring." They fully intend getting it out of hock and replacing it next week. Their subsequent failure to "pay back" promptly simply adds to the sense of guilt and indebtedness.

Most parents need to lock up valuables, cheque books, jewellery, purses and credit cards. Protect yourself. Don't tempt them. It will save a lot of heartache and resentment. I knew a grandmother who was made penniless by her addicted granddaughter. If an addict comes in your house be on guard. You might think, "Oh, she'll think I don't trust her." But it is better than risking feeling resentful after being robbed. Absolutely, I think that lending an addict money is not wise.

Lock up your booze and any pills. Family members are best to abstain from alcohol when their addict is around. If you can't do that, maybe you should look at your own potential for addictions.

Take anything your addict says like "I've got a great job" with a grain of salt until you see proof. Everyone, addicts included, wants their parents to feel proud of them. If you can stop asking questions and love the addict for being a human, that is more than helpful. Talk about good things that happened in childhood. Don't compare the addict with other siblings. Undeserved resentment can easily happen towards the siblings. That's the worst.

Your addict is not your average person. Many are like babies, very sensitive. This may surprise you. Sure, they usually look tough, but not about family. Many of us have a really soft spot for our family and children.

Don't go blabbing to all the relatives about your addict's business. Finger pointing, blaming and blackballing by siblings, aunts, uncles and cousins puts crazy pressure on the addict. It could backfire. I've seen the addict get friends together and vandalize the family home in retaliation. An organized, thought out intervention, maybe using professionals, is probably a better thing to do.

Look and act like an adult. Your kid cannot make you feel like a good person. We addicts cannot nurture ourselves or our own kids. How can we, when we're addicted, accept responsibility and act responsibly? We're not up to trying to make our parents feel good when we are half dead. Celebrate each baby step. If your kid goes into rehabilitation and doesn't graduate, celebrate the two hours she stayed.

If your addict stays longer, don't expect a big transformation. I encourage parents not to set high expectations and expect very much too soon. Unrealistic expectations can set the addict up for failure. Listen to your addict's goals. Support the healthy ones but don't insist on your addict's goals being your goals. Get your own. I spent eleven years getting addicted, smoking cigarettes and swearing. I wasn't going to stop overnight. Even though my Mom let me know my cigarette smoking and swearing troubled her, she didn't pressure me to stop. She appreciated each little step of improvement.

Parents who deny that their kid is an addict tend to live in some kind of fantasy. When their kid goes to jail they say, "My poor baby" and bail her out. They really want her out right away. They want to believe their addict when she says "If you help me this time, I'll be OK." The rescuing happens over and over. Very seldom does an addict get healthy without being in or having a program.

Don't go into despair if your addict ends up in jail. Memories of jail helped me stay in treatment. Many parents think their kid going to jail is a big family shame. It can be a blessing in disguise. Many addicts go to jail to have a rest or break from drug using. I sometimes felt relieved to go to jail for an unpaid fine. I knew I'd get some sleep and get three squares a day. Jail has probably saved many an addicts' life.

Families need to understand that recovery for the addict is the primary goal of rehabilitation, even before being with their own children. I needed to get healthy and learn how to take care of myself, before I could look after James and Danielle. My parents paid the phone bill and sent me money for cigarettes, shampoo and coffee. They supported me financially as long as I participated in the program. It took a lot of pressure off worrying about where I was going to get money for the weekend. I sympathize with families that don't have the extra money and are not able to do that. I spent three months in residence totally focussed on my recovery. Then I had three months of aftercare. The adjustment with my kids and myself went smoothly because I took the bus to visit them in London for the three months of aftercare. I suggest that people in recovery be aware of what they put their kids through and don't force themselves on the children right away. Family can help by encouraging the addict to regain custody only when she feels steady and ready.

Support comes in many forms. Always say "I love you." Keep an eye on your money and valuables. Let your addict know that you care about her and it is important she stays alive. My Mom was the only one I knew loved me. That love helped me stay alive. Now I am alive for myself and my children.

## Early signs of potential drug use...

- The people they hang out with are people you don't know. You don't know who is calling on the phone and with whom they are with. People who phone may speak strangely or vaguely.
- They will often look tired. Sleep patterns change. They are up at weird hours when others are sleeping. They're using at those weird hours.
- They withdraw from previously enjoyed activities.
- Their eating habits change. When people use marijuana they get the munchies. When they use cocaine they quit eating.
- They become secretive about where they are going, who they are with, who is calling them and what the phone conversations are about.
- They always need money. They can't explain where their money is going. How and where to get money for drugs is an issue for them.
- They are more easily argumentative.
- Young people will not introduce their new "friends" to their parents.
- For students, school grades drop and homework does not get done.
- School suspensions may happen.

# Hints for those entering the "real world"...

In the last eight years I have learned that there are some differences between the beliefs and behaviours of people who succeed in the real world compared to the people I used to hang out with on the street and in jail.

## Rights we do NOT have...

It is easy to assume you have rights that you really have to earn. Here are some rights I learned we do NOT have.

- We do NOT have the right to **always win**. If I feel offended or angry, I try to either express my opinions calmly and appropriately or walk away. If I blow it and get triggered into rage, I apologize later when I can.
- We do NOT have the right to always be the loudest and toughest. In jail the loudest and toughest got attention. In the real world you can get locked up again for being the loudest and toughest. Taking turns is important.

- We do NOT have the right to **be immediately forgiven, trusted or respected** by our children, family or community. Respect is earned and this takes time. Being tough and not being a stool pigeon won't earn you respect in the real world. What will earn you respect and trust is being tactfully honest, dependable and keeping your agreements.
- We do NOT have the right to **expect an apology from those who do us wrong**. If someone bumps into us in jail, we expect them to apologize right away. If you get bumped into, for instance, at the grocery store, don't necessarily expect an apology. Blow it off because it's not worth starting a fight and having the police called.
- We do NOT have the right to **have people give us another chance** just because we declared we were going straight. We created our own reputation and chaos and it is our job to clean it up.
- We do NOT have the right to have a good-looking girlfriend or boyfriend, wheels, a crib (apartment), a trusting parole officer and an instant cash flow. These things have to be earned and take time.
- We do NOT have the right to **a job just because we want it and need the money**. Improving your training or education will increase your chances of having the job you want. I decided to get a university degree so I can have the career I want.
- We do NOT have the right to **be congratulated for every small accomplishment we make.** Most people are acting responsibly every day at work and home. Learn to congratulate yourself with each small step and be the judge of your own progress.

## Talking in the real world...

People can tell the kind of lifestyle you lead by the way you talk. We can start to change our lifestyle by changing the way we talk.

- **Talking down to people** in a gruff and tough way is a shock to many people. Most of the people you will come in contact with are used to gentler or softer talk. Although the way we talk may sound normal and solid to us, it can be frightening to other people, like your mother. On my release date, when my mom picked me up, I talked to her just like I talked to the girls on the range. Later, after I learned more, she let me know that my language was frightening to her. It can offend people and that's not good if you want to get a job. And keep it!

- **Swearing** is a hard habit to break. It can feel comfortable but swearing can take us back to our old behaviours. There's a connection between how you talk and how you behave. I found that people automatically judge me based on how I speak. Good grammar and politeness open more doors. If I watch the *Jerry Springer Show* my cursing comes back. I get more respect if I speak calmly, appropriately and not too loudly.
- **Personal talk** in formal situations, such as a job interview or an appointment with a doctor or dentist, is not appropriate. Tommy told dirty jokes to the doctor and nurses when I was giving birth. They didn't laugh. They rolled their eyes and I felt embarrassed. Keep your sex life, your old scores, your old lady's or old man's business and how much money you make, private.
- **Notice how many times your sentences begin with "I."** "Shooting off your gate" brings attention to you but it might not be the kind you want. In the end, people might decide to avoid you. Everything is not about us. When you do choose to talk about what you believe or think, use "I."
- **Be careful about forcing your two cents' worth** down people's throats. Everyone has their own opinion and someone else may actually know more than you. Ask others "What's your opinion?" then be open to learning. Avoid telling them "That's bullshit."
- **If we are used to leading the show** or being the centre of attention we need to learn to make sure everyone gets their turn in the spotlight, even the goofs. Wait until others finish their sentence before you talk.
- **Say "Please,"** "Thank you," and "Would you mind if I...?" People expect you to check before you take something of theirs, touch them or pick up their baby. When you don't know what is OK with another person, ask. Say "Excuse me" after you burp or fart.
- **What is called "shooting the breeze"** in jail is called "gossiping" out in the real world. Gossiping gets a lot of people in trouble and can ruin friendships and affect employment.

## Getting along with others...

If we want to move up the social ladder to become a contributing member of society, learning to get along with others is key.

- When we are first released, we may judge others by our jailhouse rules, like being a "stool pigeon" or an "ass kisser." Society at-large, which we are trying to fit into does not use these rules. They are more concerned with laws, morals, fairness and safety. People deserve to be treated fairly including those of a different nationality, those with a disability or those with a different sexual preference.
- **If you don't get an invitation**, you haven't been invited. Phoning first to arrange a meeting or a visit to somebody's home is usually expected.
- **Don't call people after their bedtime**. Most people go to bed at 10 or 11 pm. Do call people that you care about, tell them you are thinking about them and ask how they are.
- **Shake hands when you meet someone new**, look him in the eye and say "How do you do?"
- **When you borrow things** ask "When do you want it back?" Then take good care of the item and return as agreed.
- **Be on time**. Many people out in the world are late but no one likes it. If you are late, people may assume you are irresponsible all the way around, especially employers.
- **When people ask you for a favour** say "yes," "no," or "I need time to think about it," in a respectful way. You do not have to do a favour for others and others do not have to do any favours for you. Don't take it personally if someone says "no" to your request. Be proud that you were willing to take the risk to ask for help. Favours need to work for both people. Check your motives when you offer to do a favour. Favours in the larger society do not mean that you will necessarily get something back, so don't expect it. Do a favour because you want to.

## Taking care of you...

Turning our lives around can be hard work. Finding a balance in mental, emotional, physical, social and spiritual health takes vigilance and commitment.

- **Asking for help** is one of the biggest challenges to making it in the real world. Learn to ask for it and then accept it. If you could make it on your own, you wouldn't still be where you are. If you don't ask, you'll stay where you are. Sometimes you have to ask different people. Sometimes you have to ask "who can help me?" to find the right person in the right place with the right information. Asking for help can feel like you are incompetent, at first. Learning to trust and whom to trust for help is hard work. At least, I had my mom for my first person to trust. Then I had a good recovery program, healthy friends and some skilled therapists supporting me. There is a lot of advice out there and not all of it is helpful. Find at least one person you can trust and start there.
- **Aim to make wise decisions**. Every day we make many choices. If we choose not to follow the rules in the real world then we better be ready for the consequences. Whether our choices are good or bad we need to take responsibility for our choices. You may need to go get help if you don't know what a wise decision is. Find that trustworthy person.
- **If you have trouble learning**, focussing your attention, have mood swings or have any physical or mental problems, check these out with a professional. Learning that I have ADD and learning how to manage it has made it a lot easier to get my life in order.
- **Don't let your anger bring you down.** Now, if ever I "lose it" I try to swallow my pride and apologize. I have flipped out when I felt betrayed, when my kids were being threatened or my recovery was challenged. Feeling embarrassed is a good sign that you want to manage your anger in better ways. Going to an anger management class is a good start to getting it under control.
- **If you have a drug or booze habit,** then a recovery program or some kind of strong support, like AA or a counsellor, is important. Drugs and booze is what got a lot of us into jail in the first place.
- **Don't beat yourself up when you make mistakes.** I've learned from my relapses. Everyone screws up now and then. Expect it, forgive yourself, learn from it and get back on track.

# 8
## ...lessons learned

WRITING LETTERS TO KELLY OVER THE YEARS allowed me to observe myself, learn and mature. I progressed in my ability to see my judgments, my attempts to control, my efforts to change her behaviour by producing guilt and, eventually, my feelings of anger and powerlessness. I felt confused as I considered the possibility of letting go of my efforts to influence and even letting go of hoping she would live a different life. It seemed like a huge risk. If I did not push for the best in her, who would? In retrospect, I taught myself how to love her unconditionally, as is. I noticed that what seemed to be most effective in our relationship was my expression of love right at the moment of contact with her. I committed myself to love; merely love. It was a big leap of faith. However, the result was a wonderful sense of freedom. I felt unleashed with a new sense of connection to Kelly.

Not to mislead the reader, I have relapses into wanting to control and make things, in my terms, *better* for Kelly and our grandchildren. I hear the words slip out of my mouth as if they were a sneeze, "What you really need to do is..." or "Wouldn't it be better if...?" If I am really thinking ingeniously I say something like "I encourage you to..." or "I would feel so proud of you if..." Well-developed habits are difficult to change, and change is worth the effort if the habits are damaging or hurtful.

In most relationships, including Kelly's and mine, there are moments of conflict and misunderstanding. Though we are reunited and appreciative of our connection, these dynamics still occur. I offer caution to the reader. Please accept our story as our sharing. Your experiences, situation and players are different than ours. For years I have not lived, and do not live, with Kelly. I imagine that for those who live with someone who is addicted, my proposed ideas could be doubly challenging. If you are involved with emotional or physical violence, then taking a break or even leaving the relationship, may be the best action. Ask yourself, "Can I retain ME, my sense of safety and my dignity in this relationship?" Notice if you can make the relationship one where you become enhanced as a person rather than becoming abused, used, or obsessed.

Also, consistent application of and adherence to the following lessons, requires repetition, integration and refinement. Perfection is an illusion and not the goal. I am a learning creature, as I expect you are. Please be kind to yourself with all new ideas, beliefs and behaviours.

Initially, through experiencing some of the worst sides of myself, I became better committed to practising my highest idea of myself. I experimented with different ways to express my concerns, my feelings, my limits, my wishes, and my love. Most of all, I increasingly became who I wanted to be. In the following, I offer some attitudes, beliefs, do's and don'ts and, dare I say, techniques. I discovered they served my intention to stay in contact, to offer emotional support, to gently influence and to express my love positively.

## Self-Exploration

Following the lessons are some questions for your reflection and use. Writing this book has been a powerful healing tool for me. I invite you to freely write your own responses to these questions as a strategy to deal with your present relationship challenges. The road to self-understanding and clarity can be achieved in many ways. Writing, perhaps in a journal, is a powerful creative and personal path to self-awareness. As Kelly and I wrote our story, we rewrote our history as we increased our self-awareness, forgiveness and healing love. You, too, can write and rewrite your lived experience.

Write naturally without imposing any rules. Do it in any way that works for you. You do not need to think hard. Thinking, rather than accessing an authentic response and feeling, may get in the way of self-discovery. Allow yourself to be free to be you. Let your frustrations, truths, feelings, ideas, hopes and pain flow onto the page and, please, be patient with yourself. May the following thoughts and questions be tools, along with your pen, to help mend and build the relationship to which you have committed your love.

# The lessons

1. Take Frustrations to Someone You Trust

2. Contain and Channel Your Anger

3. Avoid Arguments

4. Avoid Seeing Yourself as a Victim

5. Laugh at the Absurdities

6. Speak Honestly

7. Avoid Labels and Judgements

8. Catch Hope, Health and Goodness

9. Blame the Addiction

10. Establish Clear Boundaries

11. Show Love

12. Develop Spiritual Awareness

13. Cherish the Relationship

14. Cherish Yourself

# 1

# Take Frustrations to Someone You Trust

*It is the rare person with no hangups. If I play my hangups, I give them power over me. If I learn from them, I take charge of my life.*

D. Briggs

*…it is important to remember that each life drama, like every theatrical drama involves a script, and that somebody wrote that script. That "somebody" is you, under the "direction" of your parent figures, who were, of course, influenced by their own background, experience and parent figures.*

Muriel James

FAMILY PATTERNS ARE PASSED ON if not brought to awareness, examined and new behaviours introduced. Sorting out the dynamics of my family of origin provided the freedom of choice for me to develop healthier beliefs and responses. While my father had demonstrated out-of-control temper tantrums, my mother tended to martyr herself, rather than take assertive action. Unconsciously, following these extreme models of aggression and passivity created much pain and left me in self-loathing. It was a great wake-up day when I decided to develop better ways to care for myself.

Playing out the idea of what I thought *mother* to be, also had me caught. Often times we play roles that have been repeatedly described through the centuries in classic fairy tales and myths. When I could not be the "Good Mother" who graciously handles all, has clean, happy and healthy children, I became the "Wicked Mother" using my irrationally driven power to dominate. Sometimes I felt like Cinderella's wicked stepmother favouring my biological children, Ben and Katie. Taking Kelly's behaviours, choices and lifestyle less personally became important. Instead of getting control over *her*, I discovered my own personal power. A healthy and loving relationship with myself started to take shape. I learned to manage my inner responses and refrained from playing power games with Kelly. Eventually, I experienced her differently, because I was different. Kelly jokes, now that she has been in treatment and attends support groups, "Gee, my Mom has really changed since I went into recovery." She says it in jest but, in many ways, it is the truth. I sought places and helpers to support me. With safe people, good friends, and a number of effective therapists, I learned to reveal my heart's longings, share my struggles, tell my feelings, and transform my shame into self-nurturing. I spent years, before and after Kelly left home, resolving black memories from my childhood and building my sense of self-responsibility and inner peace. Joan Borysenko, author of *A Woman's Book of Life*, describes research examining the health of women. The findings provide support for what I am suggesting about caring for yourself and accessing support. Middle-aged and older women who were experiencing good health had two determining factors: they had high self-esteem and they had a caring support system.

People trapped in addictions are already in their own form of emotional chaos. The addiction is used as an escape mechanism from uncomfortable feelings and destructive internal self-talk. It is also a sign that they are deep into their human vulnerability. They are in no position to comfort or support someone else. A spouse, friend, Al Anon, minister or helping professional counsellor is the place to take your feelings of being overwhelmed.

If you decide to pursue the services of a counsellor or therapist, you need to feel understood and supported to make the best decisions for yourself. Since each person and set of circumstance is different, be wary of simple advice or quick solutions to large life issues. While counselling may feel uncomfortable at times, notice if you are treated with respect and encouraged to come to your own conclusions.

Observe if you are becoming more self-aware and accepting of your internal life and feelings. Are you increasing your ability to be in a caring relationship, firstly with yourself and consequently with others? Note if you are feeling more alive and have new ways to generate energy for yourself. Therapy is a success if your new awareness and learnings transform into appropriate and authentic action. New habits are hard to establish but the benefits are all yours. You will eventually congratulate yourself for giving yourself the gift of yourself.

Should you decide to use a helping professional, some basic inquiries are necessary. As in choosing any service, consider yourself a customer who is researching the right product for you and your situation. Ask for recommendations from your doctor, reputable agencies, friends and trusted people. Many therapists are willing to meet with you for an introductory visit. To acquire information to enable an informed decision, ask the following questions:

• What training do you have?
• How do you describe the way you work?

- How long have you been offering counselling or therapy?
- Have you had therapy yourself? If not, why not?
- How much do you charge? Is there any flexibility to your fee?
- How do you deal with crisis calls, should I feel the need to call you?

## Self-Exploration

1. What fears, hurts, frustrations or resentments do you have stewing internally about another person?
2. What past and destructive patterns are you keeping alive?
3. Of what character in a fairytale, myth, classic book or movie do your reactions remind you? How might you rewrite your character's lines or script?
4. What hurts or injuries, including those from childhood, need acknowledging and healing: emotional, physical or sexual abuse, neglect or abandonment?
5. What coping and survival mechanisms did you unconsciously develop in the past that are destructive to you and may be keeping your addicted loved one questioning your trustability: abusive language and behaviours, avoidance, minimizing, rescuing, depression, defensiveness, denial, addictions of your own (eating, exercise, sex, shopping, sleeping, work, TV, the Internet, gambling, alcohol or drugs)?
6. What support system is available in your community which could provide a safe place to examine and resolve your internal anguish? What personal goals could you work on in a support group or with a helping professional?
7. Without anyone else changing, what would you like to be saying and doing differently?

# 2

# Contain and Channel Your Anger

Those of us who are locked in ineffective expressions of anger suffer as deeply as those of us who dare not get angry at all.

HARRIET G. LERNER

*If you are patient in one moment of anger, you will escape a hundred days of sorrow.*

CHINESE PROVERB

ANGER HAS THE MOST ENERGY OF ALL the feelings we experience in our body. When in automatic rage, our body clicks into fight or flight, our hearts pound, and our nerve endings quiver. Just watch and listen to a newborn infant scream with rage when her stomach is aching from hunger. The survival of our species was once dependent on the adrenalin stimulation of fear and anger. Anger can rouse us to action. Regrettably, too often that action is unconscious, out-of-control and unnecessarily defensive.

The main belief that can activate rage is the belief that you can, and should, control another human being's behaviour and choices. That belief was so ingrained in me that repeatedly, when I received a report of Kelly's misbehaviours, I tended to react with either outrage or guilt. Both indicated my conviction that I had control over her choices. The size of my reaction was dependent on the tender or hot spots I carried from my own childhood. Lying, for instance, was an instant trigger for me. The angry outbursts were attempts to feel in control of my environment, while guilt left me feeling helpless and hopeless.

My dad's aggressive example of using his enormous amounts of angry energy in the form of exploding, kicking, smacking and yelling provided me with an unconscious template. Regardless of vowing never to act that way, I inwardly carried that template of how to express feeling angry. Reactions of violence and aggression are huge, often generational, bad habits. I discovered that noticing and tolerating my internal reactions and wisely choosing my responses were at least as much work as trying to control my outer life. At least the former was attainable. My goal was to bring balance to my internal feelings and my expression to the outside world. Burying one's feelings works no better than venting them at others. Part of my shame was that I knew that feeling angry was no excuse for hurting another, especially a vulnerable child. In some ways, feeling shame was a friend that drove me to access help and guidance.

With awareness and discipline, I developed new, constructive ways to express my intense feelings. Developing the belief that I am totally in control of myself, my thinking and my behaviours helped me to better contain my angry feelings. Over the years, I have increasingly become a self-motivator and creator of me. I see myself as not helpless, but a woman with many personal choices. When I feel angry, I tend to ask, "What does this tell me that I want?" and "What can I change about my behaviour to accomplish my goal?"

In a workshop with the healer, Gwendolyn Jansma, I was struck by a statement she made: "In a committed relationship, you are willing to feel feelings you don't want to feel, including anger, rage and fear." She went on to explain that, through our committed relationships, we have the opportunity to see who we really are and come to our most authentic expression of ourselves. I agree with her assessment as that has been my experience.

Preventive and effective management of anger buildup involves acknowledging and attending to the underlying feelings of helplessness, fear, sadness, hurt, and unmet needs. Feeling angry can be avoided and, if caught early, can be contained, managed and channelled or calmed. Self-nurturing is an action taken from the belief point of "I am in charge of my well-being." Parents are instructed by the airline stewardess to place the oxygen mask on their own faces first, so they might attend competently to their children. Likewise, is the need for parents to care for their own emotional needs so their children do not become neglected or abused. For over fifteen years, my days have been free of the shame of feeling out-of-control followed by physically lashing out. There has been much self-examination and learning since then, but I now go to bed with pleasure and pride in my conduct for the day or with a valuable lesson for the next day.

Many books and courses offer numerous techniques for managing anger before it becomes fuelled and active. Some that I have used include:

- Familiarize yourself with your body signals that potentially trigger you into inappropriate anger.
- Develop a scale from one to ten. One represents feeling mildly annoyed while ten signals extremely outraged. Learn to notice your body tension at lower levels of one and two. Then calm yourself.

- Run around the house or down to the basement and back before interacting with the other person. Physical activity releases some of the built-up energy in the body.
- Repeat an affirmation to yourself: "I am in charge of me. I am OK."
- Ask yourself what you feel underneath the anger and share that feeling. "I feel afraid." Typically under the feeling of anger is fear, sadness, hurt, grief or powerlessness.
- Ask yourself if the angry feeling is about NOW or if you are triggered into an older past and helpless place. If the latter, remind yourself that you are an adult and OK in the moment.
- Connect to your breath. Promise yourself to let three breaths go in and out of your body before taking any kind of action. Feeling angry can take over logic and, consequently, can trigger inappropriate reactions. Breathing can bring body and mind back to balance. Through regular meditation you can train yourself to breath in peace and let go of stress. This kind of internal peace does not easily become interrupted by outside circumstances. While stress in the muscles and nervous system increases the chance of inappropriate reactions, wise decisions and actions tend to be made in a state of calm.

With the development of a personal code of conduct, I have noticed I respond more and more from a position of compassion rather than one of helpless exasperation when others and the world do not do as I want nor serve me as I wish. I have learned that anger has its place and I decide where and when that place is.

## Self-Exploration

1. What are your triggers for feeling inappropriate and large doses of angry energy?
2. What have you noticed about your body when you are feeling angry? What is your internal experience?
3. Do you believe that you and others need to be punished for mistakes? How do you allow yourself and others to learn?
4. When do you notice yourself taking responsibility for other people's behaviours and choices? How do you feel when you do that? What could you choose to believe and do differently?
5. What do you tell yourself when things and people do not co-operate with your plans and wishes?

6. How would your life be different if you counted on people to live life their way?
7. How do you react to other people's mistakes, destructive behaviours or resistance to your *help*? What do you imagine that is about?
8. Have you done emotional, mental or physical harm to anyone in an angry fit? How might you make restitution with yourself and them?

# 3

# Avoid Arguments

*No one can persuade another to change. Each of us guards a gate of change that can only be opened from the inside. We cannot open the gate of another either by arguing or emotional appeal.*

MARILYN FERGUSON

WHO HAS NOT HEARD, "You can lead a horse to water but you cannot make it drink?" It took years, incredible awareness, and hard work to discipline and *change myself.* Repeatedly, I have to remind myself of how wasteful it is to do a change number on others, including Kelly.

My attempts to change Kelly's impulsive behaviours through logical arguments were fruitless. When I used "Wicked Mother" energy to argue, I inflicted pain on both her and myself. Efforts invested in controlling and dominating others, especially adults, are absolutely energy draining, painful and crazy making for all involved. To attempt to control another human being is power stealing or emotional rape.

Initially in my letters to Kelly, I tried to induce guilt about the children's lives. I learned later that these comments provided additional burdens to her personal baggage. Arguing or threatening with a heavily addicted person builds walls. For that matter, arguing can become a habit in any relationship in order to keep a *safe* distance. If you know your loved one is addicted, of course confront, and perhaps arrange an organized intervention, if you believe that would be helpful. Put in clear boundaries what is acceptable and unacceptable in your home. (Refer to Establish Clear Boundaries on page 170.) Once you have confronted the addiction, avoid putting energy into arguments or coaxing. It can make the *condemned* feel even more damned. Don't invest precious energy in manipulation and control tactics.

Engaging in discussions to prove yourself *right* makes the person who is addicted *wrong* again, and damages what is probably an already tenuous relationship. I expect you have heard the question "Which is more important, the relationship or being right?" Even before Kelly went into treatment I felt rewarded for decreasing my arguments with her about her unwise decisions, and increasing my appreciation for our improved relationship.

## Self-Exploration

1. How do you know when you are confronting problems and solving them or when you are engaged in fruitless arguments?

2. How much energy and time do you spend *trying* to change other people? What do you notice about your feelings and thoughts when you attempt to control others?

3. What control forms do you tend to use: pointing out the other's faults and mistakes, martyring with "Poor me," rescuing and overprotecting with "I'll take care of you," guilt tripping with "If only you loved me," bribing or having a hidden agenda?

4. What expectations could you release so that you might better accept what is, and who the other person is?

5. If you let go of controlling others, how might you better spend the freed up time and energy to make a difference to your own life?

# 4

# Avoid Seeing Yourself as a Victim

*The Buddha said that in this life we would experience ten thousand joys and ten thousand sorrows. He understood that suffering is a thread that runs through the entire fabric of our lives.*

WAYNE MULLER

KELLY HAS NEVER USED, NOR MILKED, the victim role as she easily could have done. She could have named herself a victim of her biological mother and father, and her previous adoptive family who all abandoned her. She could have decided she was a victim of a rough beginning with a different, ADHD brain pattern and a family and professionals who misunderstood her and let her down. Acknowledging unjust treatment is very different than wallowing in victimization. We are all victims of being born if we choose to acknowledge only the pain and not the joys. All of us have invitations to sit in self-pity. Kelly's appreciation for small blessings has saved her from playing *poor me*.

I had felt like a victim of my father's abuses until I realized he was merely passing on his own pain. Blaming him seemed like a quick way to redeem my childhood and my failures as a parent. Once I quit blaming, once I quit asking "why me?" to his anger outbursts, I was able to acknowledge my pain, feel and accept it, myself and him. He had his own journey in life and I was merely a player. I felt alone in my caregiving of Kelly. I took personally Les' lack of loving statements and minimal emotional involvement with her. Additionally, I was shamed and blamed by some professionals. Consequently, at times, I did feel like a victim of circumstances, became inert or had angry outbursts and cried a lot. I learned to look at the crappy stuff of my life, not deodorize it, and look at the options. Picking myself up, calling for help and taking some kind of action was always the cure.

Like Kelly and me, we all have the seed in us that can grow into feeling victimized. As babies we come into the world totally vulnerable and helpless. Unless we have the opportunities to acquire survival skills, indeed the capacity to thrive, we can allow present events to take us back to a state of insecurity. Sometimes I have been my own perpetrator. That is, I have victimized myself with unrealistic expectations, self-imposed put-downs and condemnation. Other times I had unrealistic expectations of Kelly and felt victimized when she didn't live up to them. Examining my beliefs allowed me to change them. I have caught myself saying, "She makes me feel so afraid." In actuality no one *makes me* feel anything or do anything or be anyone that I don't choose for myself. I make me. You make you.

Reclaiming personal power by making wise decisions, no matter how one feels, is essential for a successful adult life. Those who smile while actually feeling like a victim are called *martyrs*. They hide their pain in their belief that they will be loved through their sacrifice. However, most of us avoid martyrs. Life happens and so does pain. However, we always have the free will to choose how we respond.

The undesirable outcomes of playing a victimized role are huge. Spiritual teacher and medical intuitive, Caroline Myss, warns that identifying with being a victim and holding on to past grudges and hurts is a danger to our well-being and health. She encourages us to guard against losing our energy to meaningless ideas, to be self-responsible and to celebrate our accomplishments.

Being pro-active on one's own behalf is a great antidote for feeling victimized. So is counting your blessings. Even better is keeping a gratitude journal. Talk show host, Oprah Winfrey, recommends that each night we write five or more blessings in a gratitude journal. I have used this suggestion in times of despair and felt lifted to a view of thankfulness. "Goodbye victimization." If you struggle for your first item you may simply write "I can breathe."

## Self-Exploration

1. How did you or do you co-operate with being oppressed or victimized?
2. In what ways do you set yourself up to feel and act like a victim?
3. What old hurts are you still holding in your grudge bag?
4. What activities infuse you with feelings of excitement, self-appreciation and personal power?
5. What can you begin to do that will lead to a more pro-active pattern?
6. What are your blessings?

# 5

# Laugh at the Absurdities

*Perhaps I know why it is man alone who laughs: He alone suffers so deeply that he had to invent laughter.*

FRIEDRICK WILHEM NIETZSCHE

I GREW UP IN A CLOSE-KNIT FARMING COMMUNITY near my cousin, Donna, who was a year older than I. My aunts and uncles would put on old-fashioned pressure. "Now Patsy, you're twelve years old and Donna already spends time with a boy. When are you going to get *serious* and take an interest?" So I did. Then it was "Patsy you're fourteen already. Donna had a boyfriend a long time ago. When are you going to get *serious* about a boyfriend?" So I did. Then there were messages about becoming engaged, getting married and having children. One day I woke up with three animated and giggling children and I was busy trying to make them *serious*. Too infrequently a gleeful sound was heard in our home. How I wish I could have been serious about my parenting role, while laughing at Kelly's escapades and looking on the lighter side of life. Life is full of contradictions, surprises, exaggerations, paradoxes, and absurdities — all ingredients of humour.

Wondrously Kelly and I now laugh at her and my shenanigans, our misunderstandings, our mis-directions, our similarities, and our differences. We share some common ground in forgetfulness, she with ADHD and me with menopause. She says, "Another hereditary symptom I got from you, Mom," never missing a beat. Humour signals that pain has passed. One cannot be in an uptight state while either crying or laughing. When raising our children, I would have strep throat or flu two or three times a year; add to that, several irritated bowel syndrome attacks and an arrhythmia attack. No doubt I would not have been as ill as often if I had been relaxed enough to chuckle at what was not physically or morally dangerous or uncontrollable. I wish I had been able to laugh at the little things that did no harm to the world. Many of the painful or tragic stories we have from our childhood can be transformed into comic description. Most of us have some naughty tale to tell. With distance and a changed perspective, a humorous angle presents itself. Some of Kelly's creative solutions to her ADHD dilemmas are quite funny. Just look at the creativity utilized in some of the incidents described in the first chapter.

I encourage people in the parent classes I facilitate to laugh at mistakes that are harmless. Going back to talk about those shaming times, crying and then laughing can release months or years of shame for both parent and child. When I was a girl, my brother and his friend would wait until I rode my bicycle a third of the way down a big hill. Then they would move behind me, tapping my back bike wheel until, to their delight, I was teary eyed and as mad as heck. One morning I waited until they were ahead of me, revved my peddling power and mowed into them from an angle. In that moment I was Wonder Woman. In the next I was feeling terror! Both boys were bloodied in the ditch with their demolished bicycles. The neighbour boy's bike looked like a squished tin can. Then somehow we acquired adult help and amends were made. But my father was never told this story. For years I was afraid he would find out. Now I can laugh at a girl who, in revenge, had more power than she could ever imagine; maybe even fit enough to compete in an aggressive roller skate derby.

A word of caution about humour. Please be careful about the target. I avoid targeting Kelly or her struggle with addictions for humorous comments. That is her stuff and she plays with it well. I enjoy laughing *with* her. No one enjoys being *laughed at*, unless they are comedians who earn big payments in return.

In recent years I have developed a reputation as a fun and joyful person, actually leading workshops on increasing the play and laughter in the lives of parents, teachers, women and others. There is an old African proverb that says "If you can walk, you can dance. If you can talk, you can sing." I add "If you can admit your flaws, you can laugh at them." I tend to use gentle self-deprecation, silliness, and word plays. I'll say things like, "I'm happily married...most days." "Before I had kids I knew how to be a perfect parent. Now that I've had three children I'm thankful they're alive and I'm not a suspect." "If I'm so smart, why don't I know where I left my...I don't remember what I lost!" "I'm a seasoned woman flavoured by my children," and "I'm a greedy liver." This last statement is one that I learned from my mother who, I discovered as I loosened up, has a delightful sense of humour. She's been a great humour coach to me. The following questions might help coach you into a lighthearted attitude around your sorrows and stress.

## Self-Exploration

1. What puny irritants can you let go and perhaps laugh off?
2. How might you acknowledge your humanness and personal absurdity to your loved ones?

3. What humbling or naughty stories about yourself could you tell?
4. What are some fun and enlivening activities you could include in your routines and calendar?
5. How might you see that the real joke of life might just be your over-seriousness?

# 6

# Speak Honestly

*When I want to speak, let me think first: Is it true? Is it kind? Is it necessary? If not, let it be left unsaid.*

A SUFI SAYING

SHARING WHAT IS HAPPENING FOR YOU in an open and honest manner provides healthy modelling, keeps your fifty percent of the relationship real, and makes you emotionally accessible to yourself and to your addicted loved one. I learned a lot about myself by trying to stay honest with Kelly without pushing her away. Notice *trying*. Honesty, especially emotional honesty, is hard work. We all lose energy when we are not self-respecting and honest with ourselves. Now I can feel energy, like a plug being pulled from under me, leave my body when I am not honestly living and speaking my values. My eyesight becomes foggy, I feel sleepy, perhaps depressed. Honesty generates energy and clarity.

Between believing we have control over another person and believing we make no difference to others, is the idea that we do influence others. "Influence" means to have moral power by demonstrating personal power to live a life of integrity. Modeling honesty and care and appropriate availability can make a positive difference. The dynamic of *making a difference* requires that someone is interested or ready to receive *influence*. For many years when Kelly felt lost to us, I counselled and facilitated many people who were ready to make changes in their lives. I felt honoured to participate as a support and influence. While Kelly had no intention, or was not ready, to make healthy shifts, there were other arenas available to me to *make a difference*. Many helping professionals, including myself, have to guard against the tendency to take inappropriate credit for client successes or failures which can consequently hook us into power and control ploys. Then we are right back into that grandiose position of believing we can control someone else and her life.

Practise letting go of the belief that you can control someone else and conversely the belief that you don't matter. Speak your truth more for your own self-respect. As one of my mentors often says, "Tell your truth and let go of the results." Kelly's responses were outside of my control. My intentions and my life were mine to create. If I held on to one truth that made a difference, it was that my intention was to give

Kelly the message of, "I love you no matter what." Say what you do know about the addictive behaviours and avoid becoming an accomplice to the addiction. Free yourself to discuss what you know and how you feel. In whatever areas you can, clearly demonstrate understanding, acceptance for the person and concern about the substance abuse. Once Kelly began giving me glimpses of her addicted lifestyle, I heard things that stood my hair on end. I wanted to scream "Stop this self-destructive craziness!" That is not the kind of honesty I am talking about. I recommend a position of careful sharing of observations. Your addicted loved one is probably investing energy to present a strong, perhaps tough and false, front. Keep your side of the relationship as lovingly authentic as possible.

Apologizing is an important aspect of honesty. If you have said or done something that you regret, genuinely express it. It does not matter how long ago or how insignificant. Too many people are waiting in pain for their elderly parents, or some significant adult from their past, to apologize for an injustice. If saying, "I'm sorry. That was my wrong doing. What I said and did was more about me than you," resonates with truth, healing can happen. Healing happens for both parties, the offended and the offender. Trust will begin to develop. Although it took over twenty years for Kelly to really trust my stability, it happened. Making amends with her has helped me rest all kinds of guilt I carried for years for letting her down.

My own story with my father supports my belief that children decide there is something wrong with them when they experience abandonment or emotional or physical attacks from significant adults—especially their caregivers. Children struggle to make sense of the world. Since children perceive adults as "knowing all" the child's conclusion tends to be "I am the bad one here." Therapists such as Alice Miller, John Bradshaw, Claudia Black, Nathanial Brandon, and many others have written extensively about the destructive beliefs and abusive patterns that are passed on to the next generation. Later in life, shame, resentment, and anger become by-products for the *adult child*. How my dad treated me, and what he did to me, was passed on to Kelly—the good, the bad, and the shaming.

So, if you recall a past incident in which you imagine, believe or know you caused injury, check it out with your addict. Be honest and apologize, whether your loved one has been aching about the event or not. You have nothing to lose and potentially much to gain in relief, authenticity, and renewed connection.

Apologizing is a form of declaring personal responsibility. Too often, I learned that Kelly was carrying responsibility in the form of shame, which did not legitimately belong to her. I am sure she is not alone in this. By catching up on apologies and forgiveness, we are better able to keep on track with current conflicts. Kelly is freer now to tell me when she is struggling in our relationship. She'll say "I feel hurt, Mom. I don't like what you said," or she will ask, "Are you feeling mad, Mom?" and we will go from there.

Forgiving is the other side of the coin to apologizing. I had to forgive myself for the injustices I caused Kelly before I was able to apologize to her. I needed to understand and then forgive my father for his abuse of me before my pained and angry triggers calmed. Children do not betray adults, while many parents, regrettably, betray their children. Children are injured when they are emotionally, physically or sexually abused, emotionally or physically abandoned or when they are held responsible for their caregiver's well-being. If *it takes a whole village to raise a child*, a child is really left adrift if she does not have her caregiver providing the necessities to grow in love and capableness.

The more wounded we are, the more easily we move into defending ourselves and feeling revenge rather than forgiveness. Forgiveness takes committed work. The process of forgiveness has a number of steps. First you may need to speak your hurt and angry truth with someone safe and accepting. Privately screaming or crying may work equally well. The second step requires an intentional and conscious *letting go* of control of the other person. The final step is one of breathing with ease and experiencing peace and gratitude. There is no forgiveness that is not honest forgiveness. Your heart and mind need to be in agreement before the act of grace happens. After forgiveness comes freedom from feeling like a victim. As Caroline Myss says "Forgiving is one of the most self-centred acts you can do."

## Self-Exploration

1. How often do you tell yourself the lie "I can make her (or him) well?" What could you tell yourself that is true, and yet loving, about yourself and about the other?

2. Do you tell yourself the lie "I don't matter. I have no influence"? What is the truth?

3. In what ways might you be enabling your addict? Do you deny the degree to which your loved one is hooked by an addiction? Might you be denying the same truth about yourself?

4. What information and indicators do you have that suggest, perhaps confirm, "He or she is addicted"?

5 . What feelings of regret or guilt are you carrying that could be released with a sincere apology?

6 . Are you aware of what you have done for which someone may be trying to forgive you? What have you done that might result in someone feeling betrayed, violated or abandoned?

7. What resentments or grudges are you holding on to?

8. In what self-pitying or blaming thoughts do you notice yourself indulging?

# 7

# Avoid Labels and Judgements

*The more deeply you understand other people, the more you will appreciate them, the more reverent you will feel about them.*

STEPHEN COVEY

UNCONDITIONAL LOVE COMES WITH NO PUT-DOWN LABELS that humiliate and lessen another human being. There is a tendency in North America for parents to call their children "lazy" to encourage them to act industriously, "stupid" to encourage them to make wise decisions, and "selfish" to encourage sharing. How can a person who believes she is stupid make a wise decision? By name-calling we put our dear ones in a double bind. They will either believe us, which would be a tragedy, or challenge our position, which may be a huge emotional risk.

When Kelly was called "a juvenile delinquent," I felt twinges of guilt and dismay. "Mother of juvenile delinquent" was a sign I used to carry in my self-image. Even who we call "criminal" sends love to her mother, maybe even sends her mother a card laden with roses and a heart. Labels confine, eliminate the worth of any tender deed, and leave the branded imprisoned in a judgmental box.

Those with addictions are usually suffering from a self-concept problem already. Do not do further damage. Believe that you have more influence than you imagine. Certainly you can make a positive difference in your own life by practising the discipline of unconditional love. I had no idea, until recently, how significant and large I was in Kelly's life. There were times that I questioned whether she received my messages. The idea of photocopying my letters to Kelly helped me in valuing, sustaining, and protecting my endeavour to keep contact through the mail. I also valued the letters as a kind of personal journaling process. I was able to track my personal, emotional, and spiritual development. Some people have used a technique called *unsent letters* to work through painful relationships. Mine happened to be *sent letters*. Giving meaning to your sincere efforts can be a sanity saver. If I had written the letters for the sole purpose of changing Kelly, I might have given in to labeling and name calling out of frustration and hopelessness. My intention to create my own human and flexible label, a "committed, imperfect and loving mother" supported me. Fortunately Kelly was eventually able to see the changed mother available to her and respond.

## Self-Exploration

1. What behaviours and situations stimulate you into judging yourself or others? How might you let go of these judgments?

2. What labels do you notice yourself using in the context of those who are addicted: "drunk," "wino," "bum," "irresponsible," "lazy," "druggie," "dope head," "pot head," "pill popper," "user"…?

3. What demeaning labels, put downs or judgments do you notice yourself muttering internally: "stupid," "ignorant," "loser," "sucker," "wimp," "failure," "bad"…?

4. How is this *stinking* thinking mirrored in your relationship with others? What are the consequences of this habit?

5. After saying "Stop" to these putdowns, what healthier messages might you give yourself?

# 8

# Catch Hope, Health and Goodness

*Many individuals, have, like uncut diamonds, shining qualities beneath a rough exterior.*

JUNVENAL

*Nobody wants to be nobody. All our acts are partly devised to fill or to mark the emptiness we feel at the core.*

A. FOWLES

A LONG TIME AGO, I HEARD ABOUT RESEARCH done with convicts. Prison inmates who eventually became functional and contributing citizens reported that what gave them the power and motivation to overcome a crummy history of crime was this: for at least one year, one supportive person expressed to him the message "you are lovable and capable." Simple! And yet, not so easy.

Look for health, kindness, and awareness in your addict's words, descriptions, conversations and behaviours. I let the words "I love you, Mom" mean everything I could when Kelly said them. If she spoke longingly of her children, I would amplify her connection to them. The basic guideline here is see, hear, and translate the best. Call it thinking like an optimist if you will. I practised catching moments when I felt connected, respected, and loved by her. I learned to expand my appreciation of any sharing she offered me. When she described behaviour I considered socially unacceptable and inappropriate, I acknowledged her for telling me the truth. I wanted her to identify me as an available source of acceptance.

A whole 1990's therapy has evolved from the idea of noticing what is working well called Solution Focused Therapy. S. DeShazer and others such as W. O'Hanlon and M. Weiner-Davis are leaders in this approach. The pioneer may have been Alfred Adler, who wrote in the 1930's about encouraging desirable behaviours in children. Going back even further, Jesus said something like "It is done unto you as you believe." See *the good* in your loved one. Train your eyes and ears to see and hear beyond what is obvious in the addict. I never lost the view of our bright and lovable Kelly.

## Self-Exploration

1. What qualities, deeds, messages, and memories of your addicted loved one do you value?
2. What observations of *goodness* or healthy behaviours could you express?
3. If you are not able to see or experience appropriateness or *goodness*, what thoughts or beliefs might be shadowing your ability to do so?
4. Is fear or anger more predominant in your heart than love and appreciation?
5. How might you increase your love and appreciation quotient?

# 9

# Blame the Addiction

*It is invaluable to persons in their struggle to take their lives and relationships away from the problems that they find so troublesome.*
MICHAEL WHITE

W E LIVE IN A SOCIETY WHERE WE ARE OFTEN TRAINED to find someone or something to blame. "If only he would." "He drives me crazy." "She won't let me." "If it wasn't for her, I would be OK." "She made me do it." Targeting *something* is less damaging than attacking someone. Michael White, an Australian therapist, developed the idea of *externalization*. He learned that some Chinese peasants view their children's mis-behaviours as the result of wicked spirits invading the child and fighting the child's naturally sweet nature. The caregiver then administers a liquid tonic to expel the evil invader from the child. The innocent child is protected and experiences no personal attack. However, the child and parent believe the "demon" has been destroyed and changed behaviour is the result. Viewing troubling behaviours as monsters or dragons that have consumed your loved one can help depersonalize your interaction. Modern day troubles are symbolically described in our culture's fables, stories, and myths, and so might be the answers.

I felt quite excited after learning about this way of thinking. I began to put externalizing phrases in my letters to Kelly. From this perspective, I was free to tell her how frustrated and afraid I felt without blaming her. Kelly's addictions had *robbed*, *stolen*, and *attacked* her and all those who cared for her. I felt free to express strong and angry feelings about all that had been *taken away* — many of the joyful, healthy, creative and responsive aspects of her that I missed and had grieved. I offered to support her in *fighting*, *standing up to*, and *challenging* this "external" *enemy* that had *cheated* so much from her, me, her children, and all those who proclaimed a caring concern for her well-being.

If ever you sense that addictions are the *leading force* in your loved one's life, determine your limits of helping. Define *help* as *get well*. This is not the same as rescuing that ends in wasted money and effort. Rescuing can often lead to feeling used and resentful. Defining the difference between rescuing and helpful support may be a complex assignment but may relieve guilt in the end.

## Self-Exploration

1. Do you tend to blame yourself or another when things go wrong? What are the main beliefs that support your blaming?
2. How would your relationship change if you stopped blaming yourself, or the other, and directed your angry energy at *the addiction*?
3. How would you experience a person who is challenged by addictions if you imagined him or her consumed by an outside force, similar to being invaded by a flu virus?

# 10

# Establish Clear Boundaries

*We come to see ourselves as clearly separate from others, yet not too distant, and if our boundaries are intact we have a sense of well being.*

ANNE KATHERINE

SAYING "NO" TO BAIL MONEY FOR KELLY was one of the toughest messages we ever gave. "Enabler" is a term used in the addiction field to define someone who makes it conveniently possible for a person hooked by any kind of addictive habit to continue. Enabling is their addiction, their way of avoiding their pain. They focus on their addict. Some enablers lie to cover up the addict's behaviours, rescue with money or excuses, or simply deny there is a serious problem. We eventually learned not to enable Kelly. Les and I talked extensively and concluded that we wanted to present a clear message of "we do not support your present decisions involving drug and alcohol use and its consequences." We wanted to respond in the most responsible way.

In retrospect, I imagine that a number of times when we *helped* Kelly pay for rent or new starts, we were inadvertently enabling. I still wonder if we were naive or uninformed or a mixture of both. Certainly, earlier on, we were not aware of the depth of Kelly's addictions.

Deciding what your values are, and what behaviours are acceptable and unacceptable to you, is important. Clarify your intention and your boundary. Then your messages will be clear and less emotionally driven.

## Self-Exploration

1. Are there circumstances, with your addict, when *no* is difficult for you to say? Where and when?
2. What values have you established that receive your financial or energetic investment: health, peace, home, family, responsibility, purposefulness, orderliness, discipline, respect, human rights, tolerance, justice, compassion, honesty or love?
3. Which, if any, of your values become challenged or skewed when you are in contact with your addicted loved one?

4. What values and boundaries do you need to clarify and then declare to protect your integrity?

5. How might you end the following sentences?
   — From now on I will...
   — From now on I will not...

# 11

# Show Love

*When the satisfaction or security of another person becomes as significant to one as one's own, then a state of love exists. So far as I know, under no other circumstances is a state of love present regardless of popular usage.*

H.S. SULLIVAN

*The need for supporting core self-esteem doesn't end in childhood. Adults still need 'unconditional' love from family, friends, life partners animals, perhaps even an all-forgiving deity. "No matter how the world may judge you, I love you for yourself."*

GLORIA STEINEM

SUPPORT YOURSELF IN HAVING YOUR MAIN INTENTION to be a demonstration of love. Let go of the belief that you have any power to change another human being. Because everyone longs to feel loved, it has a powerful influence, yet it loses its potency if it hangs on an expectation of desired change. This theme has been repeated before in this book. It is the theme! It was and continues to be one of my main life lessons. Kelly is one of the most stubborn people I have ever met. It takes a lot of effort on her part to change her mind. I have a stubborn streak, as well. Darn it all! I sent "I love you" over and over regardless of her reluctance to receive the message.

If you are loving to get something back, you may need to ask, "what kind of love is this?" Become a source of love, not a tit-for-tat dealer in the commodity of *feeling good*. Of course, there is a place for conditional love. That has to do with acceptable and unacceptable behaviours. Make statements about boundaries and conditions for preferred behaviours. We need to clearly communicate the behaviours we will not support or tolerate and what we are prepared to do about breaches of trust and agreements. At the same time, it is essential for the survival of the relationship to remember that we are not human DOINGS but human BEINGS. The BEING can always be loved. The task is to separate the deed from the doer.

My belief is that human beings deserve unconditional love because they exist. Our dog that peed when she became excited, provided no household help, required regular walks and daily grooming, was fed and loved for JUST BEING. Sure, she was reprimanded for her piddle spots, but her unique lovableness was never questioned. Regrettably, many people are not given the same message of irreplaceable value.

The beginning of Kelly's acceptance of help and support came when she really believed she was loved by me. Then she began to see the lovableness in herself. It was as if she finally saw the reflection of my message. I sent "You are loved" and she was, eventually, able to see "I am lovable." It took over twenty years for that message to be sent, refined, sent again and again until it was truly unconditional. Finally it was received, and anchored with trust. She allowed it to change her life! I remain grateful.

## Self-Exploration

1. In what ways and in what situations do you struggle to accept "what is" and "who is?"
2. What unacceptable behaviours trigger you into feeling hopeless, angry, afraid, hurt, rejected or attacked and unable to love the actor?
3. How might you begin to separate the doer from the deed, the person from the behaviour, your unconditional love from your conditional love?
4. What messages of unconditional love and conditional love could you create? Examples of unconditional love include "I love you" and "I miss you." Examples of conditional love include "I feel disappointed that you are still using drugs" and "I support this decision."
5. What elements of self-love are lacking in you that interfere with your ability to offer loving acceptance to others, particularly your addict?

# 12

# Develop Spiritual Awareness

*There is nothing to get out there. A full life is about using your spiritual qualities*
*of joy, peace, creativity, health, beauty, and especially love. All is available within.*
CAROL CARNES

*The body is the physical expression, the Self is the individual psychological expression,*
*and the soul is the expression of our essence as it merges with universal consciousness.*
J. ROSENBERG

FINDING A SPIRITUAL PRACTICE HAS PROVIDED DEEPER MEANING and an inner place of comfort for me. For most of my life I have not been a faithful devotee of any particular belief or path preferring to call myself a *spiritual seeker*. There were times when I felt quite out of control with Kelly and had no internal means of centring or calming myself. I required outside help and support. In many ways therapy led me to the experience of my spiritual self. Years ago in Sarnia I was in a therapy group where I learned a guided meditation that went something like this:

*I have a body but I am not my body. My body houses all the necessary organs*
*and tools for my human life but I am more than a body.*

*I have a mind but I am not my mind. My brain is a wonderful tool in helping*
*me master pertinent parts of the external world. My mind can be creative and*
*think of new possibilities based on what I know of myself and the world but I*
*am more than my brain's functioning.*

*I have feelings but I am not my feelings. Feelings are internal messages about*
*what is working or is not working for me. They inform me of my personal truth.*
*Sad or hurt feelings tell me I do not have what I want. Feeling angry tells me I*
*have energy to pursue what I want. Afraid tells me I am at risk of losing*
*something I value, while feeling happy gives me the message that I have what I*
*want. Feelings are very important and I am more than my feelings.*

*I have hopes and wishes, but I am not my hopes and wishes. These give a*
*sense of a possible future. However, I exist only now in the present moment.*

*Therefore, at my core, I AM a spiritual being.*

For some people, spirituality has become a fad these days and, in all probability, a healthy one. For too long I believed, like many others, that acquiring material things and a trouble-free life was supposed to create happiness. Life is more mysterious and intangible than objects and an easy ride. Happiness is overrated. I enjoy crying during a sad movie. I grew to appreciate my feelings, including feeling disappointed with my lack of success in relating to Kelly. I watched myself. I learned how those disappointments had to do with patterns of exerting control. As my *witness* self-developed, I more compassionately noticed my reactions to Kelly. I changed and so did my perceptions of Kelly. Eventually, I experienced her as a perfect spiritual being with her behaviour and addictions in the background, rather than the foreground.

Some days I would torment myself with questions. "What difference do I make? Who am I really? What is the meaning of my life?" These are questions many of us ask in an effort to make sense of our human existence. The questions are worth exploring. One answer is to see yourself as a mere light of energy, energy that exists to create your own unique life. Remembering who you really are and who your addict really is, can soften life like a velvet cushion on a hard chair.

At some point, I was able to observe myself, Kelly, and our family like watching a video movie. I have found that nurturing the idea of a watchful and caring witness provides a nonjudgmental part, or spirit if you will, simply noticing life as it unfolds. In the Buddhist tradition this activity is called "mindfulness." The caring witness can be a source of unconditional love for yourself and your addict. All is well from this spiritual perspective of watching the drama of you and your loved one in relationship.

Like many other people, I have experimented with a range of spiritual practices: meditation, attending Sunday services, journal writing, contemplative walking, Gabrielle Roth dance movement, watching TV's *Oprah*, yoga or sitting in my mother's garden. Some weeks I am more disciplined than others but always the time invested in centring myself with a divine source and idea has been rewarded with calm. An added benefit is that a spiritual practice is probably one of the most preventative measures you can develop to manage anger. Peace is always possible inside yourself if nowhere else.

I have shared pieces of my spiritual awakening. My overarching invitation herein is for you to find your own path to inner peace and tranquility. Embrace and develop a faith that supports you in all that you are and can be in this lifetime and beyond.

## Self-Exploration

1. What belief about life have you developed that internally supports you in the good and bad times?
2. Like favourite foods that nurture your stomach, what have you noticed brings peace to your heart and soul?
3. What thoughts and beliefs bring you a feeling of serenity?
4. What meanings have you created around the pain you and your addicted loved one have experienced?
5. What have you named the part of you that compassionately notices: "Spirit," "Soul," "Witness," "The Divine," "Higher Power," "God"…?

# 13

# Cherish the Relationship

*Where you stumble, there your treasure is.*
J. CAMPBELL

*If we learn to see our relationships as the wonderfully accurate mirrors they are, revealing to us where we need to go with our own inner process, we can see much about ourselves that we would otherwise have a great deal of difficulty learning.*
SHAKTI GAWAIN

NOW APPRECIATE ALL THAT I HAVE EXPERIENCED with and through Kelly. This most demanding relationship has been one of my finest gifts. I was once told that you can view the people in your midst as lovers who support you or as teachers who challenge the best in you to come forward. Another perspective is to experience each message as either an expression of love or a cry for love.

Through my *motherly* commitment and struggle with Kelly, I discovered more about myself than by any other means. I learned that my primary relationship needs to be with myself; Kelly was like a mirror. I realized my reactions to her behaviours were a reflection of what I needed to take personal responsibility for — a signal to look at myself. Our relationship became a means to self-revelation, especially the parts of myself that needed healing. Each incident with Kelly — even those when she seemed lost in a dark shadow — was a chance to stretch and learn something about my own potential. If I failed myself, then I failed her. If I could accept and love myself, I could do the same for Kelly. As our relationship improved, my gifts were then reflected. I learned not to give up hope in my ability to love, no matter what. I consider myself blessed.

## Self-Exploration

1. What opportunities has this challenging relationship created for you?
2. How have you grown as a person?
3. What have you learned about yourself, relationships or life, itself?
4. What could you, and will you, put on your gratitude list for this relationship? What are some of the hidden and visible blessings?

# 14

# Cherish Yourself

*"I want to know and care about myself. I want to feel high energy and a sense of freedom." That's my nutshell description of the essence of high self-worth.*
SHARON WEGSCHEIDER-CRUSE

CHERISHING FEELINGS, THOUGHTS, AND BEHAVIOURS can become a habit. They require discipline and commitment. Spending time, money, and energy on therapy made a huge difference for me. Through wise therapists, teachers, and friends I received the message to claim my self-worth, listen to my body wisdom, identify and heal my childhood wounds, and live in a conscious and self-responsible way. I was fortunate to have had a number of skilled therapists in my life.

Increasingly, I learned about the information my body holds about my personal history. I recalled childhood memories of my dad that held pain. However, I began to see that, as an adult, I could use that pain to motivate me to make other choices. The past became my background and not an excuse for present behaviours. Additionally, I began to better appreciate my body as the container of my personal and spiritual power. I had a storehouse of resources that I needed to treasure and nurture.

The more I attended to myself and did not take action driven out of anger, guilt or wanting to control, the more effective I felt about, not only my contacts with Kelly, but my life as a whole. As self-acceptance, self-forgiveness, self-care, and self-respect developed, so did my bond to myself.

Learning to love myself was probably one the hardest tasks on the road to unconditionally accepting Kelly. Though Kelly was quick to forgive me for errors in raising her, I first had to forgive myself. For years I had wrestled with the fact that I had been physically abusive with Kelly but not with Ben or Katie. Self-forgiveness was a necessity for me to really connect to Kelly from a non-defensive and freely caring position. Kelly's diagnosis of ADHD was of some help in alleviating my shame for this discrepancy. Also, before developing hope and possibility for Kelly, I needed to create it for myself. The good news is that all these healing processes will never be lost. They are lifelong treasures no one can take from me.

It is probably impossible to really understand someone else. To understand yourself requires a tremendous amount of work. I am continually amazed about how much I don't know about myself as I allow myself to unfold. How could I have possibly understood what was going on for Kelly when I knew so little about my own reactions and ingrained patterns?

Conversely to the axiom "you can change and control no one" is "no one can change or control you." I did not like many of my behaviours, but I was comfortable with them, stuck in a complacent rut. Changing myself was hard work. Realizing how, as an adult, I was responsible and in charge of myself took repeated practice. Some days I still quaver, looking for someone to rescue me, to tell me what to do and how to succeed. I have learned to more wisely choose behaviours and words to enhance my own self-worth and consequently have opened the door to loving connection with Kelly.

## Self-Exploration

1. What don't you like about yourself? What are your personality weaknesses: stubborn, critical, pessimistic...? How might you soften your perception of these features and develop some compassion for yourself?
2. What have you done for which you need to forgive yourself?
3. What do you like about yourself? What are your personality gifts and strengths: creative, patient, respectful, funny, intelligent...?
4. What are your capabilities? How might you celebrate and share them?
5. What good deeds do you feel proud of?
6. Who loves and supports you? What are some of their most encouraging and caring messages?
7. Are there things you say to yourself, excuses you give yourself to stop getting the help and support you deserve?
8. From where and whom could you more readily request and accept help?
9. What ways might you nurture yourself and increase your self-esteem?
10. What nurturing affirmations and self-care messages could you and will you give yourself?

Some examples:
- I am loveable just the way I am.
- I am capable.
- I can take care of myself.
- I can trust my own wisdom.

- I can say "no" and "yes."
- I can feel afraid and take action, anyway.
- I am safe.
- It is OK to make mistakes.
- I can have fun.
- I can feel all of my feelings and express them.
- I can change by noticing how I think, believe, ponder, and feel.
- My truth is important.
- I deserve to be seen and heard.
- I can choose and be responsible for my choice.
- I can feel weak or strong and ask for help.

# Conclusion

**M**ANY DISTURBING EXPERIENCES CAN BECOME GIFTS. When I think of the pain and tension Kelly and I have moved through, it deepens my appreciation of her, myself, and existence itself. I have joy and love in my life that I could previously never have imagined. The idea of creating my own vibrant life as a key tool to relationship connection was my biggest awakening. As Kahlil Gibran wrote:

> *Your joy is your sorrow unmasked.*
> *And the selfsame well from which your laughter rises was oftentimes*
> *filled with your tears.*
> *And how else can it be?*
> *The deeper that sorrow carves into your being, the more joy you can*
> *contain.*

I have surrounded myself with supportive people only to find myself a supporter of others. By increasing my self-care, I have developed a repertoire of cherishing words and deeds. Now that Kelly has returned to our lives, I have much to share with her. It comes, mostly, with ease. I feel so pleased and proud that I have offerings that help sustain her and others, that I originally developed to support myself. All the years Kelly was away, I grew and strengthened. Now those tools and inner knowledge are available to the world and, particularly to Kelly, to support her, a piece at a time, as she is ready.

## A special message to the parents of addicts

To those committed parents of adult children stolen by addictions, please remember the following:

- Only you can decide what role you will play in your child's life without future regrets or resentments.

- Only you can decide how much of "living your own life" is the role of being a mother or father.
- Only you know how much of your time, money and energy you can "safely" invest in your child's well-being with no expectations for a positive outcome — while holding onto hope for the best.
- You, more than anyone else in the picture, know your child — the person buried under the addictions. You probably know if you are being used or are genuinely being asked for healthy support.
- Moments you've been in the light with your child — in childhood, at play, in your arms — have allowed you to know your child far deeper than those voices who name-call your dearest "addict."
- If your child trusts you above all others, you may be the only thread to the possibility of recovery.
- Only you can decide what you need to do so that in five or ten years you can look back and say, "I did the best I could with what I knew and what I had."
- Only you can decide what kind of motherly woman or fatherly man you will be. The rest is minor and/or is out of your control.
- When your child is lost in the darkness of addictions you need to protect yourself.
- If and when your child turns away from addictions you can be (not "need to be") available in the light to hold that dear hand.
- Being in the light with your child is still your decision.
- Your child has been stolen from you, maybe repeatedly by drugs, and will probably have a lifetime vulnerability to using drugs. You know all of that…and you know much more. Most of all, you know why you love your child.

Speaking of love, I celebrate you for all the internal turmoil you are allowing yourself to feel and I commend you for your willingness to use your brilliant mind and your tender heart to make wise and caring decisions for yourself and your dear one. There are no right or wrong decisions unless it is not a good fit for you or causes harm to others.

# Bibliography

## Favourites from Kelly's bookshelf

Carnes, P. (1989). *A gentle path through the twelve steps: For all people in the process of recovery*. Minneapolis, MN: CompCare Publishers.

Casey, K. (1992). *Each day a new beginning: Daily meditations for women*. Center City, MN: Hazelden

Estes, C.P. (1992). *Women who run with the wolves: Myths and stories of the wild woman archetype*. New York, NY: Ballantine.

Hallowell, E.M. (1995). *Driven to distraction*. New York, NY: Simon & Schuster.

Hallowell, E.M. & Ratey, J.J. (1994). *Answers to distraction*. New York, NY: Pantheon Books.

Kelly, K. & Ramundo, P. (1993). *You mean I'm not lazy, stupid or crazy!* Cincinnati, OH: Tyrell & Jerem.

Mamori, I. (1992). I *want to tell you about my feelings*. New York, NY: William Morrow and Company.

Morrison, M.A. (1989). *White rabbit: A doctor's story of her addiction and recovery*. New York, NY: Crown.

Nelsen, J., Iner, R. & Lott, L. (1992). *Clean and sober parenting*. Rockline, CA: Prima Publishing. **Note**: new title is: *Positive discipline for parenting in recovery*.

Powter, S. (1997). *Sober: Staying that way: The missing link in the cure for addiction*. New York, NY: Simon & Schuster.

Solden, S. (1995). *Women with attention deficit disorder*. Grass Valley, CA: Underwood Books.

Spungen, D. (1983). *And I don't want to live this life*. New York, NY: Ballantine Books.

Wegsheider-Cruse, S. (1987). *Learning to love yourself*. Deerfield Beach, FL: Health Communications.

# Favourites from Patricia's bookshelf

Adams, J. (2003). *When our grown kids disappoint us: Letting go of their problems, loving them anyway, and getting on with our lives.* New York, NY: Free Press.

Adams, K. (1990). *Journal to the self.* New York, NY: Warner Books.

Bailey, L.J. (1984). *How to get going when you can barely get out of bed: Every woman's handbook for dealing with depression and frustration.* Englewood Cliffs, NJ: Prentice Hall.

Bradshaw, J.E. (1992). *Homecoming: Reclaiming and championing your inner child.* New York, NY: Bantam Books.

——— (1987). *Healing the shame that binds you.* Pompano Beach, FL: Health Communications.

Brandon, N. (1987). *How to raise your self-esteem.* New York, NY: Bantam Books.

——— (1971). *The disowned self.* New York, NY: Bantam Books.

Briggs, D. (1977). *Celebrate yourself: Enhancing your self-esteem.* New York, NY: Doubleday.

Callwood, J. (1986). *Emotions: What they are and how they affect us...how we can deal with the way we feel.* Garden City, NY: Doubleday.

Cameron, J. (1992). *The artist's way: A spiritual path to higher creativity.* New York, NY: Putnam's Sons.

Canfield, J., Hansen, M.V., & Hewittt, L. (2000). *The power of focus.* Deerfield Beach, FL: Health Communications.

Clarke, J.I. (1989). *Growing up again: Parenting ourselves, parenting our children.* San Francisco, CA: Harper & Row.

Claypool, J. (1994). *Wise women don't worry: Wise Women don't sing the blues.* Encinitas, CA: Cornucopia Press.

Clinton, H.R. (1996). *It takes a village: And other lessons children teach us.* New York, NY: Simon & Schuster.

Covey, S.R. (1989). *The 7 habits of highly effective people.* New York, NY: Simon & Schuster.

Cousins, N. (1979). *Anatomy of an illness as perceived by the patient.* New York, NY: Bantam Books.

De Shazer, S. (1985). *Keys to solution in brief therapy.* New York, NY: Norton.

Dreikurs, R. (1953). *Fundamentals of Adlerian psychology.* Chicago, IL: Alfred Adler Institute.

Eisler, R. (1987). *The chalice and the blade: Our history, our future.* San Francisco, CA: Harper & Row.

Fillmore, C. (2004). *Against all odds: When ordinary people do extraordinary things.* Toronto, ON: Elias Press.

Frankl, V.E. (1959). *Man's search for meaning.* New York, NY: Pocket Books.

Gawain, S. (1993). *The path of transformation: How healing ourselves can change the world.* Mill Valley, CA: Nataraj Publishing.

———. (1986). *Living in the light: A guide to personal and planetary transformation.* San Rafael, CA: New World Library.

Gil, E. (1983). *Outgrowing the pain. A book for and about adults abused as children.* New York, NY: Dell Publishing.

Goleman, D. (1995). *Emotional intelligence: Why it can matter more than IQ.* New York, NY: Bantam Books.

Grabhorn, L. (2000). *Excuse me, your life is waiting.* Charlottesville, VA: Hampton Road Publishing.

Harpur, T. (1992). *God help us.* Toronto, ON: McClelland & Stewart.

Hendricks, G. & Hendricks, K. (1993). *At the speed of life.* New York, NY: Bantam Books.

Houston, J. (1996). *A mythic life.* San Francisco, CA: Harper Collins.

James, M. & Jongeward, D. (1973). *Born to win: Transaction analysis with gestalt experiments.* Reading, MA: Addison-Wesley.

Jampolsky, G. (1979). *Love is letting go of fear.* Berkeley, CA: Celestial Arts.

Katherine, A. (1993). *Boundaries: Where you end and I begin.* New York, NY: Simon & Schuster.

Keys, K. (1975). *Handbook for higher consciousness.* Coos Bay, OR: Living Love Publications.

Klein, A. (1989). *The healing power of humor.* New York, NY: G.P. Putnam's Sons.

Kopp, S. (1972). *If you meet the Buddha on the road kill him.* New York, NY: Bantam Books.

Kushner, H. (1983). *When bad things happen to good people.* New York, NY: Avon.

LaRoche, L. (2001). *Life is not a stress rehearsal.* New York, NY: Broadway Books

Lerner, H.G. (1985). *The dance of anger: A woman's guide to change the patterns of intimate relationships.* New York, NY: Harper & Row.

Miller, A. (1986). *Thou shalt not be aware: Society's betrayal of the child.* New York, NY: First Meridian Printing.

Mountain Dreamer, O. (1999). *The invitation.* San Francisco, CA: Harper Books.

Muller, W. (1992). *Legacy of the heart: The spiritual advantages of a painful childhood*. New York, NY: Simon & Schuster.

Myss, C. (1996). *Anatomy of the spirit*. New York, NY: Harmony Books.

O'Hanlon, W.H. & Weiner-Davis, M. (1989). *In search of solutions*. New York, NY: W.W. Norton & Company.

Orsborn, C. (1986). *Enough is enough: Exploding the myth of having it all*. New York, NY: G.P. Putnam's Sons.

Paris, T. & Paris, E. (1992). *I'll never do to my kids what my parents did to me*. Los Angeles, CA: Lowell House.

Provine, R. (2000). *Laughter: A scientific investigation*. New York, NY: Penguin Group.

Ram D. (1971). *Be here now*. New York, NY: Lama Foundation/Crown.

Ram D., & Gorman, P. (1990). *How can I help?* New York, NY: Alfred A. Knopf.

Richardson, R. (1987). *Family ties that bind: A self-help guide to change through family of origin therapy*. Seattle, WA: Self-Counsel Press.

Rosenberg, Jack L., Rand, M. & Assay, D. (1985). *Body, self, and soul: Sustaining integration*. Atlanta, GA: Humanics Limited.

Rosenberg, J. L., & Kitaen-Morse, B. (1996). *The intimate couple*. Atlanta, GE: Turner Publishing.

Roth, G. (1987). *Maps to ecstasy: Teachings of an urban shaman*. Mill Valley, CA: New World Library/Nataraj Publishing.

Sark. (1998). *The bodacious book of succulence.* New York, NY: Fireside.

Satir, V. (1976). *Making contact*. Berkeley, CA: Celestial Arts.

———. (1972). *Peoplemaking*. Palo Alto, CA: Science & Behavior Books.

Schaef, A.W. (1992). *Women's reality*. San Francisco, CA: Harper San Francisco.

Scholten, T. (1999). *Attention deluxe dimension: A wholistic approach to ADD*. Calgary, AB: Scholten Psychological Services.

———. (1999). *ADD guide book: Comprehensive, self directed guide to addressing attentional concerns in adults & children*. Calgary, AB: Scholten Psychological Services.

Sher, B. (1994). *I could do anything if I only knew what it was*. New York, NY: Delacorte Press.

———. (1979). *Wishcraft: How to get what you really want*. New York, NY: Ballantine Books.

Simon, S. (1988). *Getting unstuck: Breaking through the barriers to change*. New York, NY: Warner Books.

Steinem, G. (1993). *Revolution from within: A book of self-esteem*. Boston, MA: Little, Brown and Company.

Stone, H. & Winkelman, S. (1989). *Embracing ourselves*. Mill Valley, CA: Nataraj Publishing.

Thich N.H. (1991). *Peace is every step*. New York, NY: Bantam Books.

Tolle, E. (1997). *The power of now: A guide to spiritual enlightenment*. Vancouver, BC: Namaste Publishing.

Wooten, P. (1996). *Compassionate laughter*. Salt Lake City, UT: Commune-A-Key Publishing.

Zelinsky, E. (1991). *The joy of not working: How to enjoy your leisure time like never before*. Edmonton, AB: Visions International.

# Appendix I
## ...educational affirmations

THE FOLLOWING IS REPRINTED WITH PERMISSION from *HELP! for Parents* by Jean Illsley Clarke. Also available from the author at 16533 – 9th Avenue North, Plymouth, MN, USA 55447.

**Being, Stage I, 0 to 6 months**

- I'm glad you are alive.
- You belong here.
- What you need is important to me.
- I'm glad you are you.
- You can grow at your own pace.
- You can feel all your feelings.
- I love you and I care for you willingly.

**Doing, Stage II, 6 to 18 months**

- You can explore and experiment and I will support and protect you.
- You can use all of your senses when you explore.
- You can do things as many times as you need to.
- You can know what you know.
- You can be interested in everything.
- I like to watch you initiate and grow and learn.
- I love you when you are active and when you are quiet.

### Thinking, Stage III, 18 months to 3 years

- I'm glad you are starting to think for yourself.
- It's OK for you to be angry and I won't let you hurt yourself or others.
- You can say no and push and test limits as much as you need to.
- You can learn to think for yourself and I will think for myself.
- You can think and feel at the same time.
- You can know what you need and ask for help.
- You can become separate from me and I will continue to love you.

### Identity and Power, Stage IV, 3 to 6 years

- You can explore who you are and find out who other people are.
- You can be powerful and ask for help at the same time.
- You can try out different roles and ways of being powerful.
- You can find out the results of your behavior.
- All of your feelings are OK with me.
- You can learn what is pretend and what is real.
- I love who you are.

### Structure, Stage V, 6 to 12 years

- You can think before you say yes or no and learn from your mistakes.
- You can trust your intuition to help you decide what to do.
- You can find a way of doing things that works for you.
- You can learn the rules that help you live with others.
- You can learn when and how to disagree.
- You can think for yourself and get help instead of staying in distress.
- I love you even when we differ; I love growing with you.

## Identity, Sexuality and Separation, Stage VI, adolescence

- You can know who you are and learn and practice skills for independence.
- You can learn the difference between sex and nurturing, and be responsible for your needs and behavior.
- You can develop your own interests, relationships, and causes.
- You can learn to use old skills in new ways.
- You can grow in your maleness or femaleness and still be dependent at times.
- I look forward to knowing you as an adult.
- My love is always with you. I trust you to ask for my support.

## Interdependence, Stage VII, adult years

- Your needs are important.
- You can be uniquely yourself and honor the uniqueness of others.
- You can be independent and interdependent.
- Through the years you can expand your commitments to your own growth, to your family, your friends, you community, and to all humankind.
- You can build and examine your commitments to your values and causes, your roles, and your tasks.
- You can be responsible to your contributions to each of your commitments.
- You can be creative, competent, productive, and joyful.
- You can trust your inner wisdom.
- You can say your hellos and goodbyes to people, roles, dreams, and decisions.
- You can finish each part of your journey and look forward to the next.
- Your love matures and expands.
- You are lovable at every age.

# Appendix II
## ...definition of terms

**acid**: hallucinogen; LSD

**bricks**: brick shape, chunks of hash

**coke**: cocaine

**crack**: type of free base cocaine which is smoked

**crack pipe**: small pipe used to smoke crack

**chickening**: seizure due to an overdose

**cocaine**: white powder drug

**free basing**: is creating crack cocaine. Powdered cocaine is mixed with baking soda and heated until the consistency of oil. This mixture sticks to anything metal and then hardens

**fried**: very stoned

**gold seal**: term used to describe the quality of hashish

**hash**: made from marijuana plants (resin from flowering part of female plant)

**hash oil**: cooked down hashish mixed with isopropanol (rubbing alcohol), which becomes a tary-like substance

**heroin**: narcotic made from a type of poppy plant

**hooping**: stashing or hiding in the vagina

**hot knives**: method of inhaling hash using two knives which have been heated to singe small quantities of hash

**jones or jonesing**: painful withdrawal while seeking more drugs

**kife**: bad drugs

**methadone**: drug used in the treatment of heroin addiction

**narcotic**: regulated drugs that are also used for medicinal purposes to alleviate pain

**OD**: to overdose or to take too much of any drug which the body cannot break down quickly enough

**pot**: marijuana

**rock**: crack cocaine; a free base cocaine in rock form

**shooting up**: using a needle to ingest a drug
**speed**: a stimulant; amphetamines
**toke**: a puff of a drug
**weed**: marijuana leaves and/or bud; the flowering part of the female plant

Thank you to Peter Baylis and the volunteers of the Youth Drug Line, Distress Centre/Drug Centre of Calgary, Alberta, Canada

# An Invitation

**M**Y GOAL WAS TO GIVE MY LOVE AND CHALLENGE with Kelly meaning by turning it into a support offering for other people. Kelly then participated by adding her perspective. We are interested in your experience of reading our book. Please send us a note if you would like to share any of your thoughts, feelings or questions with us.

Blessings to you.

Patricia

**Patricia Morgan**
**1411 – 25A Street SW, Calgary, Alberta  T3C 1J8**
**phone: (403) 242 • 7796**
**e-mail: patricia@lightheartedconcepts.com**
**website: www.lightheartedconcepts.com**

# Personal notes

# About the Authors

PATRICIA MORGAN BEGAN LIFE IN RURAL ONTARIO where she met and married her teen sweetheart, Les Morgan. After careers as an Early Childhood Educator and Parent Education Facilitator, Patricia returned to school in 1984 to complete a masters degree in Clinical Psychology. She has worked as a family therapist, career counsellor, women's group facilitator and consultant to parents of acting-out teenagers. In 1999 she became a Certified Integrative Body Psychotherapist and has a counselling practice in Calgary, Alberta.

In addition to counselling, Patricia speaks across Canada about family dynamics, women's issues, self-esteem, and the value of light hearted living. She has also compiled the book, *She Said: A Tapestry of Women's Quotes*.

As an accidental writer, she is grateful for the gifts that have come from revealing the story of her relationship with her daughter, Kelly. Patricia is also mother to Benjamin and Katie and grandmother to Kelly's three children, James, Danielle and Eric. Patricia is vibrantly alive and happily connected to her loved ones...most days.

KELLY MORGAN ENTERED THE RECOVERY PROCESS OVER EIGHT YEARS AGO and has participated in a number of programs. Since her Attention Deficit Disorder diagnosis she has become informed and better skilled at managing it. After Kelly's youngest, baby Eric, is a little older, she intends to complete her university education.

Kelly has become a source of support to others who are entering the recovery process or who are beginning to make healthy changes in their lives. While there are some days she still struggles with life challenges, Kelly most often celebrates her new accomplishments and blessings with her three children, extended family and AA friends.

Another book by Patricia Morgan

# She Said: A Tapestry of Women's Quotes

compiled, annotated and introduced by Patricia Morgan

*She Said* calls women to find their own voice. Women of any age love it as a gift of appreciation— for Christmas, Valentine's Day, Mother's Day, anniversaries or just to say, "You matter."

*She Said* gathers together a wide variety of thought-provoking, normalizing and witty remarks by women. Included are Nellie McClung, Maya Angelou, Mary Walsh and many other famous, infamous and otherwise unknown wise and wisecracking women. The collection is organized to reflect the transitions and challenges in women's lives. Each of the 20 categories includes Canadian content and a special space for personal and reflective writing. Readers will be stirred by more than 350 insightful quotes and invited to discover their own "say-so." The cover design features eight delightful and spiritually-inspired images by Calgary artist, Chandra Gilbert.

## A few sample quotes:

Never retract, never explain, never apologize — get the thing done and let them howl. NELLIE McCLUNG (1896 – 1951), Canadian suffragette and author.

A bird doesn't sing because it has an answer, it sings because it has a song. MAYA ANGELOU, b. 1928, American entertainer, poet and author.

I don't do much falling down anymore. But if pushed, I'll do anything to get a laugh. MARY WALSH, b. 1953, Canadian comic.

# ORDER FORM

- *Love Her As She Is: Lessons from a Daughter Stolen by Addictions* has supported and given direction to many people concerned with loved ones susceptible or challenged by addictions or other troubling circumstances. Purchase it to help that person who is hurting and seeking a way to love while maintaining clear limits.

- *She Said: A Tapestry of Women's Quotes* is a thoughtful gift for expressing appreciation or affection to a sister, daughter, mother or friend.

*Telephone orders*: **(403) 242 • 7796**
*Fax orders*: **( 403) 240 • 1964**
*On-line orders*: **patricia@lightheartedconcepts.com**

*Mail orders*: **Light Hearted Concepts**
**1411 – 25A Street SW, Calgary, Aberta, Canada  T3C 1J8**

Please forward the following quantity of book/s:

*She Said* @ \$12.95 + \$3.05 S&H per copy = \$16.00 × =

*Love Her As She Is* @ \$21.95 + \$3.05 S&H per copy = \$25.00 × =

Name:
Company:
Address:
City:
Province/State:
Postal/Zip Code:
Telephone:
E-mail:

Total enclosed including S&H charges:

Please make cheque payable to *Light Hearted Concepts*

# ORDER FORM

- *Love Her As She Is: Lessons from a Daughter Stolen by Addictions* has supported and given direction to many people concerned with loved ones susceptible or challenged by addictions or other troubling circumstances. Purchase it to help that person who is hurting and seeking a way to love while maintaining clear limits.

- *She Said: A Tapestry of Women's Quotes* is a thoughtful gift for expressing appreciation or affection to a sister, daughter, mother or friend.

*Telephone orders*: **(403) 242 • 7796**
*Fax orders*: **( 403) 240 • 1964**
*On-line orders*: **patricia@lightheartedconcepts.com**

*Mail orders*: **Light Hearted Concepts**
**1411 – 25A Street SW, Calgary, Aberta, Canada T3C 1J8**

Please forward the following quantity of book/s:

*She Said* @ $12.95 + $3.05 S&H per copy = $16.00 × =

*Love Her As She Is* @ $21.95 + $3.05 S&H per copy = $25.00 × =

| | |
|---|---|
| Name: | |
| Company: | |
| Address: | |
| City: | |
| Province/State: | |
| Postal/Zip Code: | |
| Telephone: | |
| E-mail: | |

Total enclosed including S&H charges:

Please make cheque payable to *Light Hearted Concepts*